S T I M

T0347178

STIM

AN AUTISTIC
ANTHOLOGY

EDITED BY

LIZZIE
HUXLEY-
JONES

unbound

First published in 2020

Unbound
6th Floor Mutual House, 70 Conduit Street, London w1s 2GF
www.unbound.com
All rights reserved

Text design by Ellipsis, Glasgow

A CIP record for this book is available from the British Library

ISBN 978-1-78352-902-5 (hardback)
ISBN 978-1-78352-904-9 (paperback)
ISBN 978-1-78352-905-6 (ebook)

Printed and bound in Great Britain by Clays Ltd, Elcograf S.p.A.

3 5 7 9 8 6 4 2

For us

With special thanks to Carole Edmond
and Ellie Roberts for their
generous support of this book

Contents

Introduction

Lizzie Huxley-Jones

I have always been searching for myself in books. I found shadows, glimpses, parts of people who felt like me at least some of the way – Roald Dahl's Matilda Wormwood came closest. It wasn't until I was twenty-six that I realised I had been looking for autistic people, like me.

I remember the exact moment; it was a Sunday, around eight in the morning, sunlight dappling on my skin as my partner snored softly. A friend had just been diagnosed so, being the person that I am, I began researching autism. There is something eerie about unexpectedly seeing your life on a page, and as I read blog posts and articles I realised I was reading about myself for the first time. Eighteen months later, my partner and I found ourselves curled up on a Saturday night after a long week, reading an email confirming that I was, indeed, autistic.

In the in-between, when I was working out whether I could or should get a diagnosis, I read. I fell back on the safety of books that I had sought as a child, devouring everything I could get my hands on. I was often elated, euphoric even, realising that people felt deeply in the same way I did.

But I started to notice something else, a trend. The majority of what I read was not *by* us, but *about* us. TV and film kept showing me a particular type of autistic person – good at maths, socially inappropriate, male, white. Sheldon Cooper in *The Big Bang Theory*, or Dustin Hoffman's character in *Rain Man* were the models, and also who everyone's minds leaped to when autism was brought up. The dialogue around autistic people in some cases seemed so bleak – we were either 'problem children' or unemployment statistics.

This didn't match up with the wide variety of people I had met in the eighteen months of discovering my autistic self, nor the people I have met in the years that followed. The saying goes in our community that if you've met one autistic person, you've met one autistic person; our individualities make us just as unique as non-autistic people, beyond the diagnostic criteria that link us. Given that current estimates suggest one in a hundred people in the UK are autistic, you certainly know several autistic people, whether you know it or not. They are deeply passionate people, who bring magic and colour to my life on a daily basis, who stick together to help each other through crises, who brim with excitement and happiness when allowed to be themselves.

I tweeted something along these lines, wishing for an anthology of autistic voices that could show me some of the creativity held within our community that would also be the reflection I so sorely longed for. I quickly got a reply from Julia

Kingsford, publishing powerhouse and champion of autistic voices, telling me I should do it, and that's how *Stim* began. If you're reading this book, it's possible you have followed its journey from tweet to the book in your hands, but if not, know that it was born of love and frustration and hope and sheer admiration for all the people who ended up in its pages.

The tide has started to turn in the two years since that idea, and that tweet. Autistic people are more often allowed to be spokespeople for their own communities at all levels, and we see passionate prominent autistics like Greta Thunberg, Chris Packham and Jack Monroe championing for a better world for everyone. We've had documentaries presented by autistic people exploring the communities of undiagnosed adults, and Netflix specials hosted by autistic comedians. But there is still that backlash, the snide comments about us being too much, too strange, too unlikeable; we still have a way to go. I hope that this book can be a small part of this positive change, this push towards greater acceptance and understanding of autistic people. Reading breeds empathy, and what autistic people need, ironically, is greater empathy from non-autistic people.

While the book contains a range of ages, genders, sexualities and life experiences, the majority of contributors to this book are white. Autism in people of colour is dramatically under-represented and under-diagnosed, as criteria built around white cis boys and institutional racism combine together to delay diagnoses for people of colour. It is quite possible that this, plus my own whiteness, contributed to a lower proportion of pitches from people of colour. If you wish to read more about autistic people of colour, I fully recommend the anthology *All the Weight of Our Dreams*, edited by Lydia X. Z. Brown, E. Ashkenazy and Morénike Giwa Onaiwu.

You can find out more about autism in the Resources section at the back of the book (page 191), which also has a little background information on why we chose the title *Stim*, and a further reading list.

I hope that by exploring the work and lives of the eighteen people in this book, you, dear reader, will feel more connected to autistic people. The essays, short fiction and art in this book represent a wonderful range of creative expression from some of the most exciting established and new voices in the arts. *Stim* is a showcase of the tremendous, and often untapped, talent in the autistic community. While contributors were told their pieces did not specifically have to be about autism, you will see many of them touch upon facets of the autistic experience, reflecting how many of us see our autisticness tightly integrated with the rest of our selves. Thank you for supporting us, and for reading.

MARACA

gemma williams

Content note: Descriptions of sex

I'm pouring steaming water into bucket counter-clockwise, widdershins, and singing 'Summertime' to the ruby-blood mixture below.

I have been out in the lanes. I have made my fingers cold and inadequate, wettened by the reddening of haw blush.

I am making a love potion for you.

It has become a ritual of mine; these lanes, this time of year. Rabbit, guffawing pheasant, bat, swallow – the Longman gazing down and Vanessa's long shadow from up the way.

I haven't lived here for several years now. Well, two years. Two long years filled with many lifetimes. I know this because I have one bottle left. 'Come Hither', kept waiting in a dark cupboard between honey meads and this year's batch of emergent sloe gin.

'Come Hither, Berwick to Selmeston Way, 2013'.

Blackberry and lavender wine. Now I have lavender growing in my garden. Aside from the bindweed it is the only thing really that has flourished here in this shady, tangled city lot.

If I lie down in my garden and let the bindweed make me its own, would you, firstly, ever hear of it, but, supposing you did, secondly, care?

I have collected these fruits for your arrival but I suspect they will never cross lips nor work themselves on your finer self: You are growing tired of the novelty that was me, I can feel it.

I want to dance with you more than anything. I don't know why you're asking me, now, if I want to dance, or how I'm meant to answer a question like that, because you're obviously only asking me so that I can decline, so I can excuse myself . . . But we came here to dance. I flew here to dance. You told me you burned to show me your culture, its spirit, its music, to dance with me. I'm wearing sandals even though it's still winter here. I've dressed carefully. I'm wearing the string of beads you gave me to make myself elegant. I've eaten through two courses of fish. I hate fish.

I can hear the tourists scraping chair legs against the tiles, rising amiably, and there are still the footsteps left over from the Tahitian dancers of the show and a salsa is playing and I have been practising salsa in front of the laptop to online tutorials and willing myself forward to this moment, when you'll take my hand, and lead me up from the table, guide me lightly to the centre of the

6

room, and adrenaline and fear will flood me, and I'll start to feel my cheeks flush, and my pulse play in my neck, but you'll smile and start to step with the music and

I'll follow

and you'll be happy that I am answering you

and you'll be happy that I came to see you

and happy that I can dance despite my Englishness.

Now you're mouthing the words to songs I don't know and raising one thin eyebrow and bobbing your head side to side like a man contentedly feigning enjoyment and I can see the tiredness beneath the mirth and I know you don't have it in you. You're asking me if I want to dance and I just can't imagine what the words are to answer that kind of question where the only responses I can give are sad or lies or a loud scream at your performance of having fun.

Nobody is having fun.

And when, days, weeks later you are reviewing the evening, you will recall that we did something extremely fun but that I sat sad and sullen while you poured expensive cultural experiences into my wineglass.

I can see the lines of those future thoughts being erected along cable poles as we sit here, telegraph wires drafted outwards from the now. You can't see them yet, but I can. Trajectories are easy to predict.

So I am mute, I try to smile. You are smiling. We are smiling, People are smiling. I can't touch anything real to hang my muteness on as it is all in my own mind and that is how you have caught me. I can't play those games where people allude to one thing or act 'as though' when clearly there is another thing entirely, but this happens all the time and the fact that I am failing again at being happy as is expected of me and wished for me drags the murkiness up around my throat and I keep smiling, prettily, stupidly, because my eyes must look like deep holes driving into the half pineapple and melted ice cream I couldn't force myself to eat.

With my souvenirs I light a fire – the papers, the photos, the tickets, embruled in purple smoke condensing against the cool night air as tumbling lilac rain down around the beehive – I'm trying a new method of communication.

I am shaken to my core. That's an expression people use when they are deeply perturbed by a usually unexpected, upsetting event. But I made love to a mountain, a volcano. I let him enter me and quake within me and now the mountain itself has been ricocheting, oscillating between off and on, a binary dance of place – here, there, there, trembling – of course I should be shaken here in the garden, at night, hunched over coughing embers in another hemisphere, back the right way up but still feeling full of the mountain that at this moment is convulsing and trembling.

When I remember this I am no longer sad. I have not lost the man, the lover, the anything, because the lover was also the mountain and the mountain is still within me, shaking in symmetry with its other self, inverted and massive on the other side of the earth, muting my peculiarities into insignificance by its mass.

I part my legs. The leather between them is sand-soft and warmed with sunlight. I grip with my thighs and feel the softness of the flesh that young girls aspire to eradicate, flattening against the bulk that also compresses my vulva, and curls upwards behind my coccyx.

You said you were 'improving your bronco service'. It was only a typo – you meant your 'bronze' service tour-guiding but I preferred the mistake; it's more accurate.

I watched a film on the return flight about love across distances, plane trembling below me with the turbulence. Emotional and social terrain rather than geographical, but distance is distance. The young man in the film was a bull-rider. I like to draw upon these connections when I'm trying to make sense of why you aren't talking to me at that moment. It's like the naming of constellations by observing the essential shape they describe. So this constellation is a bull and

I am clenching the saddle with my soft thighs and hoping, like the young man in the film, that this bull is a considerate one.

Both consultations I have made with oracles have said the same thing: *Bumpy ride. You'll be shaken around* (I think of your earthquakes). *But this is your lesson. This is your opportunity.* To weather the storm. To ride the bronco, to shake with the mountains and meet with unknown gods.

I wish to meet with unknown gods. I tire of the fey and whimsy of the English countryside and city life. I feel your tremble and roar a plumb line beneath me and my womb answers *yes*. I can weather your quakes and rumbles, your heaves and sighs. Your static moments, your withdrawals and uncertainties I take and sit steadfast and uncurl my hair from its twist, find my centre of gravity and await your furore.

If I were pregnant, and I had the beginnings of your son inside of me, if I was secreting God's gift to you, the son you have been praying for, if the honey cap had slipped or I'd got my timings wrong, would you want to talk to me then?

All you could say was *please, no chat*. I don't know what that means and I am supposed to be a linguist. But the use of the tongue is not the same as directing neurons around training circuits where it's imperative that each red-helmeted, chemicalised concept doesn't motor into another. I don't have the brain for churning out crash-course motorcyclists and I don't understand why you aren't talking to me unless maybe you think you might have a son harbouring himself in ruby velvet within a woman who sleeps under your roof, if not beside you, or the promise thereof.

I am a day late but that will be the apprehension and the knowing that once I let go, once I let her flood . . . I will be releasing any cells you left behind within me. Any memory of you will be bleached away like moonlight on bones.

Cock and hen. The city is abuzz. Fish guts still soften the underside of my snakeskin boots, the taste of *avalons* leaning into my tongue. Earthy. Solid. Unexpected.

She is young. Buoyant with a shy joy. A fresh bud, beautiful, pink and frilled, pretty as a doll. White flag flaring. Methodical steps, counting the moves as she sashays side to side. Her eyes are upturned crescents, patent black shoes flashing the dimming sunlight back upwards to the high colonial windows, ricocheting around the square, tallied with the sound of the *cueca,* ushered forward from a cackling public-address system on small wheels.

He, his boots wink and writhe with a mastered subtlety. Spurs click upon the cobbles, proud leather mollified by age creaks paternally around the Bright, Young One.

-*Daughter,* his fast steps cry, *Daughter, I am your father. I have always been your father. But I am your lover too- for I am the cock and you are the hen- and we only have these two roles*

11

*to play- //**twirl**// -and I have provided for you- //**stamp**// -and I shall continue to provide for you- //**stamp**// -long after you have become a mother yourself, after you have chosen your mate- //**twirl**// -but we only have these steps- //**aha!**// -and I must teach you them- //**spin**// -so let us dance, daughter, spin for me, show the sun you appreciate his warmth, show the land you appreciate his strong back, show you father you can receive by giving-*

The rhythm composes itself and the gathered street crowd murmur appreciation and clap with glee. The girl, the virgin bride is beaming. The parents step forward from the ring and take her hand, guide her back into anonymity. The old cock grins a toothy smile up at the sky and bows from the waist.

This room has become my sanctuary.
It is not unpleasant and, moment by moment, its taupes and greys and simplicity soften into a room that can be home, while suspended upside down in another world.
I haven't known quite what to make of this place yet, this city yet. Its tongue is fat against my ear and its streets incoherent. But I am with him once more. Another hotel room. Perhaps we will only ever make love in rooms designed for tired tourists and other pairings like ours; refugee lovers clinging to sheets with furtive wails as we are tugged apart by those waiting for us in our homes. Or at least, waiting for him in his home.

I am spending many hours gazing at the mountain,
sometimes with my eyes shut because it is not the retinas I
am trying to embrule with it – I wish for its impression to
lean into my consciousness. I need this mountain, there is
drought within me that only it can fill.

I need to be small again.
To be towered upon, silenced by a broad stoicism and a dense
weight of mass. I can feel it behind the closed curtains as he
uncurls beside me in sleep, it easing into me.
And in the morning, when he leans over me and coos into
my ear, moving inside of me it is the mountain I feel
entering, slowly, a gradual osmosis of form,
man as mountain, mountain as man,
felling me methodically, systematically, silently.

pozo

I see both of our faces in the water.

I am reflected there, beside him, at the bottom of the well,
and I wonder . . . does that mean that I belong here now?

Has her face impressed itself upon the water beside his?

We opened the hatch only very briefly, late-morning winter
sun flashing behind two heads soft with the knowing that we
are in love, my face, at least, wet with the tears that fell with the
shocked encounter with a tree, faded with aged and abandoned
pomegranates. This is the kind of excess here; this is what is
superfluous and unwanted.

I hear the chickens still, picking up the corn behind me and for a second we are at the bottom of the well together. A pinhole snapshot pressed into the blood of the land that has been calling to me since he sat before me that first day, skin dewy with dark charm.

I am here, I tell the water. *I have come*. Go tell it to the mountains, go creep about the roots of the trees and feed me up into their fruits of next year. Let me permeate you as you have permeated me.

You are more beautiful than anything I could have imagined. Because you are everything I have tried to imagine. I have sought you out along the fox-ways and the forest-ways. I spent the night buried deep in the earth trying to find you and I was choked back up with the dawn chorus left wanting. My home. I have been waiting for you desperately, until I was too tired to wait any longer.

Yet here I stand, you before me, as if it were nothing, as if you were always only ever just around the corner, as if every pomegranate, every walnut, every lemon or fresh egg had only ever been a facsimile clue, a series of arrows pointing me back towards home, a home my soul had flung itself far away from, landing in another world where my only option was to live muted, tongue-tied, confused and alone because that, that which I see around me in that place is not home, it does not make sense to me, I am inherently alien and the vast love poured upon me by people whose paths cross mine only serves to make me feel more alone. For something has been lacking, something has been absent and calling to me though the hedgerows and the tarmac and the pomegranates and the walnuts at Christmas-time and now I am transported here, and I can see my house, low and yellow, and the garden cackling with life and I only want to fold myself into this mountain and never leave. This is my soul's land and my soul's people and my heart is too full with the knowing that I belong here at the bottom of this man's well, feeding upwards into his fruit, coursing under the mountain, sinking deep into the roots of the grove, reflected here for eternity.

This is my favourite time of year. I hear people muttering around me that the wind is whipping up, too soon, too early, the summer ending prematurely . . . but

I love the wind.

These streets, deadened, static in the heat, they become alive and everything dances along the tarmac. Tendrils of russet and gold and ruby shards pirouetting along the kerbside like nebulae, and at night, while I lie in my bed, I think of the pozo and I hear the cueca and the tree outside my window whispers light through holes in the bamboo screen beside my bed and the wall is lit up with shadow puppetry like when I was a child and I couldn't get to sleep and would spend hours telling myself faint stories against the orange breath of the nightlight.

And on the classroom wall, behind the student, raindrops sat upon a far window, backlit by afternoon sunlight, cast yet more shadows of thousands of pairs of cueca dancers.

With the wind come spiders; there are spiders everywhere. Spiders in the beehives, spiders in the garden, spiders in my boots. And outside my window a spider is ricocheting in the wind, and as she swings she spins, and as she spins out her silver threads she is singing into the wind. She is dancing with me across this pane of glass, and the strings she makes are the strings of a harp playing a cueca, a tarantella, and the garden outside is an orchestra of harps playing cuecas and I can hear them all and I think – it has been a long time since I played.

You are quiet with me today. The spider outside my window hangs still in the fine rain, reduced to a gross happenstance of exoskeleton, no longer a dancer. I awoke with a headache after numerous bad dreams, my soul twitching with unrest, imagining myself breaking our 'mutual agreement', resenting that fact, then even in dreaming having the wherewithal to realise that it was not me doing the breaking.

I am reverberating on the far end of a humming wire, bobbing upon your sea changes. We work like that and you are once more a family man in the family home and for all your good intentions I know you are back in bed with her even if just to appease the children and would it be so hard to

seduce you in the night? Lay a soft, warm arm about the hulk
of your shoulders? Climb your mountain range as you
slumber, you perhaps not even realising it is her stroking your
sleeping back as you dream of me entwirled amid your limbs?
but I realise all of this and I am kept from peaceful sleep
and when I wake this morning, drawn, the spider does not
even acknowledge me. Today is not a good day.

I wonder – did he feel something too? The other one? They
told me later that he had pounded a frantic salsa beat into an
amp stand, with his fists, unprovoked. Did something in him
know? Did flares shoot out from our convulsing abdomens,
ribbons of elated bowel, and prod them both at the very same
moment? He, in a basement bar, concrete, below a Victorian
station in the south of England,
    she,
        black hair licking her forehand damp with wild sweat,
small eyes folded even smaller below the crossed arms of
her eyelids, the top lip damp too, the children at school,
the mother in the adjacent room, ochre paint flaking,
coffee pot hissing ignored, her licking her lip . . . *waiting
. . . waiting . . . it will be soon* . . . maracas are beginning
to play, he is moving his hips and cooing as a dove, this
moment she has been waiting for, for years, for a lifetime,
since before they were married and a boy at school
curled shouted insults that she had a moustache across

the courtyard, pear blossom was falling, the sun was high, she had a graze on her knee that prickled with the salt of her sweat, other girls laughed – and she knew: all men will be bastards, and all girls coquettes – jiggling, giggling, maracas and now the coffee pot is erupting onto the stove top and burning dark black rings onto its surface, coagulating into an acrid mound while ribbons gurgle out of its mouth and he is ejaculating into the jerking, bleeding embrace of a braceleted figure with soft-focus eyes.

I like looking at it, not just because it is beautiful, which it is (each bead is unique and delicate and bold and light) but because it is proof that somebody saw me, and understood me, and knew exactly what I was and exactly what I needed without me saying a word. Someone saw, someone cared. Someone brought me back to life with a string of lavender lepidolite that I couldn't accept on first proffering as it seemed such a weighty gift and I am sensitive to the weight of gestures, and yet it was as light as a hollow bone and brought with it the soul I had forgotten to be.

How it was so easy for someone from another world, a stranger, to see in me all of the things I'd allowed to be degraded and sullied and lost amid a hubbub, things invisible to most of those around me, I don't know, but there are many things about all of this that I can't fathom and if wearing a string of tiny lilac beads can bring me such peace then maybe I could start talking to 'God' instead of the houseplants after all.

I cried to my sister for half an hour in the rain in the airport car park before I could return to the van. Steam rising up from the concrete floor, my choked voice echoing small from rain-smeared, reinforced glass. Back in the van I opened up all the windows to let some new air in. I finished the fruit he'd left on the dashboard for me. I rarely eat fruit. Then again, I rarely wear things around my wrists or fuck in the afternoon or eat galettes of French chocolate naked on my floral bedsheets. Rarely do I smoke either but I light up a thin menthol cigarette and listen to loud static from the portable cassette player's tinny speaker. Everything is new. I think I love him.

maracas

/then/

the phone hummed like a rash, stuffed behind the wastepaper bin in the bathroom.

I don't know how she could possibly have known. Witchcraft, perhaps,

or espionage.

the fluoro from the hallway grinning up to the foot of
the bed

mute in the otherwise dark of the room, crimson fingerprints and elbow smears quietening down now, inquisitive: How could she possibly know?

his face fascinates me. it is both unbelievably kind and mischievous in turns with a softness I hadn't expected to find. his cheeks rosy and high, a mountain boy grown into slick-membered man from whom the burden of fast-moving large numbers and a surge of youthful latin blood have removed the frontal portion of his animal-black hair from his scalp.

everything about him is soft, from his cooed ululations to the spirit-crease around his soft-lashed, soft brown eyes to the oft tenderness of the probings of his '*motivation*', thrust softly upon me while soft fingers softly hold mass.

I haven't felt the dull weight of peace like this for too long. a string of delicate beads of semiprecious stones whisper into my wrist, naked like the rest of me turned under the shade. it was so tiny when he handed it to me, I hadn't thought it would fit but it has shrunken me with its spell of calm until here I am, a woman of subtlety and fragrance, delicate and shining against—

/the rash in the bathroom is murmuring with the hiss of maracas,

maracas wound up too tight,

small beads of bone and animal droppings rattling inside taut skin. maraca, maracas, mararararacacaca/

the tongue is the only thing which is rough. its sounds, its movements are soft but the tongue itself is rough as sand, a pebble pushed into my mouth like a peppermint. the taste captivates me as does the face captivate me as do the nose, the eyes, the fingers and the smell. it is enough to take me away. I could hammock myself in this smell . . . and yet the maracas in the bathroom are chattering again. that she could know is impossible, as insane as the sound of cicadas chirruping and maracas hassling from a hotel bathroom but she is there, listening in, accusing, hissing through plastic door and incandescent strip and stained bedsheets and crackling through the crashing of brown-skinned waves and delicate, fragrant murmurings and it is my phone that is shaking now, a message from an unknown, foreign number, with letters spelling out a single word:

m a r a c a

All is still now. His mouth, his eyes, all falling backwards. *I know this number. It is my wife. 'Maraca' – it means 'whore'.*

He has a wife.

The Lost Mothers

Rachael Lucas

I hope there won't be many more mothers like me. I'm from the lost generation – the women who grew up with the sensitivity to noise, the overwhelming need to escape from social interaction; the clumsy, awkward, complicated ones. The quirky ones. The ones who stood on the sidelines at school and in social situations, wondering why everyone else seemed to know the rules for life. The last generation – I hope – of women who grew up undiagnosed, not knowing they were autistic.

I grew up with a strong sense that I wanted to have four children – not two, because I didn't want them to feel the fierce sense of comparison I experienced throughout my childhood. I wanted to create a horde, a brood, a family unit. My childhood felt oddly precarious – we moved house and country several times, so I didn't have a sense of being rooted. I wanted my children – my imaginary children – to have a sense of home. I wanted meals around the kitchen table and a sense that they would always have somewhere to come back to. If I had that, I thought, perhaps I'd feel rooted and solid and lose the sense of dislocation I'd felt all my life. So I married young and had my first child in my late twenties. Once I had a ring on my finger I felt like I had proof that I was a functioning member of society. Look, I would say to myself as I spun it around for comfort, I'm like everyone else now.

I wonder sometimes how I would have approached motherhood had I known I was autistic. Would I still have forced myself to go to parent and baby classes, where I struggled to make polite conversation and came home worn out and drained of energy? The sensory overload of crowded baby clinics, where humming bright lights and other screaming children would give me a migraine, was torture. My favourite moments were walks in the woods, where we would stamp along in the silence, looking at the wildlife and stopping somewhere quiet to eat a picnic. I'd scoop them up in my arms and kiss their damp and muddy little faces, and smell their delicious skin. They were sensory heaven. But then there were days when I was frazzled and over-touched, desperate for an hour alone to sit and read in silence. I learned my own coping methods – if I strapped everyone into car seats and went for a drive, they'd fall asleep and I could have a precious hour of just staring out of the window at a lay-by somewhere.

In other ways, though, the humdrum daily routine worked well for me, as a creature of habit. Children thrive on routine, the books said, and I could give them that in spades. Up, dressed, breakfast, a walk into the village, feed the ducks . . . it made perfect sense. And then the yearly patterns of school soothed me – the same songs every year at harvest festival, the wonky handmade Christmas cards, the end-of-term summer fete – they gave the year a comforting shape.

I approached motherhood with the same methodical process as I had everything else: soak up every bit of information first, and then see what happens. If something didn't work, I'd read and research, then try again, because the answer – I'd worked this out before – had to be that I didn't know enough. I picked up a book on attachment parenting and realised that the instinctive child-led method made sense to me. Carry your baby, they said. Keep them close, hold them in your arms. The trouble was that my firstborn would only sleep if left alone in a crib, lying peacefully for hours and wriggling to escape if I tried to carry her in a sling. I felt like I was failing because she would only settle if she was left alone in silence, not realising that she was probably as overstimulated and exhausted as I was.

She was perhaps eighteen months old when I started to realise that her behaviour wasn't the same as her peers from my antenatal group. I was (being honest) cross and slightly disappointed that when we went to toddler music class she'd lurk in the corner, not mixing with the others, quietly clacking a single castanet. To start with, I wanted my child to be everything that I wasn't, because childhood for me had been a series of failures. I was too shy for kindergarten, too self-conscious to make friends. Sometimes it was physically painful to speak. I felt as if everyone else had read the rules and I didn't know how to be a person, and here was my own child, who seemed to be cut from the same cloth. She was perhaps two and a half when I happened upon an article on autism.

I thought how interesting and strange it was that so much of it made sense – but my child was a girl, and the article didn't mention girls. There was nothing back then online about autism in girls, so I put it to one side. A brief chat with our health visitor told me that because she didn't line things up, my daughter couldn't be autistic. Meanwhile, I suspected from very early on that her younger brother had attention deficit hyperactivity disorder (ADHD). How was my mental health? the health visitor asked, the inference being that I was worrying unnecessarily about my children. Another child, two years later, and then another. They were so obviously neurotypical – meeting milestones on time, playing with toys in a completely different way – that I knew I wasn't imagining things.

My eldest daughter started nursery school and the staff suggested there was something different about her, but her father was horrified by the idea there was 'something wrong' (his words) with her. Nothing was done. Life carried on. I loved the routine and the order and the feeling of making a family, ignoring the fact that the marriage I was in was unhealthy. Like many autistic people, I didn't realise that the situation I was in was harmful. I had a nice house, four beautiful children, a garden full of flowers and a vegetable patch. I had two children who I'd learned needed something more than everyday parenting – they needed someone in their corner, explaining that no, they didn't like birthday parties because they were loud and stressful and overwhelming, and that they were never going to be the kind of children who won prizes at school for being straightforwardly obliging and easygoing. And as they grew up, my uncompromising parenting of them made me begin to question the compromises I was making in my own life. Why would I stand up for them at school and tell them they should believe in themselves, and yet put up with treatment that made me feel small and scared and insignificant?

I see my motherhood experience as having two parts – before, and after. I left the marriage when my youngest was four and the eldest eleven. Nothing was different – I'd been a single parent in all but name for a long time – but everything changed. Before I'd been too afraid to stand up and demand a diagnosis for my daughter ('she's just obstinate and badly behaved; there's nothing wrong with her'). I'd doubted myself and wondered if there *was* something wrong with me. Was I attention-seeking? Was I imagining things? I watched her struggle at school as she hit the age of ten, when the children she'd played with for years seemed to shift in preparation for secondary school. Something in my memory stirred, and I remembered the moment when I, too, found that my friends weren't interested in playing ponies or colouring in. I talked to friends I'd made online who had daughters who were going through the same thing. Was it just our imaginations? How could we all be feeling the same way?

The family home that had mattered so much to me was sold, and we were on shifting sands. But we survived. In time we moved to the seaside, I met my now husband, and we found a school where they listened and agreed that yes, there was every indication that she was autistic. Things began to change. My son was diagnosed with ADHD and his life was transformed with medication. And in the process of getting an official diagnosis for my daughter, the pieces started to fall into place. The reason I understood how she felt and could help her to navigate school and social situations was because I'd been there myself. I understood social overload and how it felt to be completely consumed by an interest. When she told a pushy teacher where to go and marched out of the classroom when she felt overwhelmed, I felt a secret sense of pride that she could express the feelings I'd had growing up.

Looking back, so much of my parenting has been informed by my autism, but for the first ten years I didn't think anything about the choices I made. They were instinctive, on the whole – I knew that there were elements of my childhood I wanted to replicate – but it has been a process of making mistakes, learning, relearning, pattern-matching and finding ways through the maze, which is pretty much how life went for the first forty years, until I was diagnosed at the same time as my thirteen-year-old daughter.

I don't think my parenting changed with my diagnosis. I mother them instinctively – my children say their friends think I'm oddly lax about things that their parents worry about, and strict about others. I don't care if they want to leave a social situation early because they've had enough, because I often feel the same way. When they were little, birthday parties were a unique sort of hell. It took time to realise that my children didn't appreciate them either – part of the complicated tangle of unmasking a lifetime of socially accepted behaviour. Everyone loves parties! We all love socialising! Except, no. Most of my family find it exhausting and stressful.

The relief of realising that we can say no and the world won't end has been huge. We've found a way to live that lets everyone in our house feel as if they're heard. Extended family members might find it odd that we celebrate birthdays the way each child chooses, rather than in the socially acceptable cards, singing and cake manner, but every family has its eccentricities. 'I'm over-peopled' is a valid excuse to leave a social situation in our house, and I'm as grateful for it as they are.

I came to motherhood convinced it would be the answer, and it raised – and continues to raise – more questions than I could ever have imagined. As my children grow – the eldest is almost twenty, the youngest nearly thirteen – the patterns of school life have faded away. They need me, but in a different way. I hand out school uniforms and ask them to go to the shop when I'm too frazzled to cope with the noise and chaos of the supermarket. I help them deal with the friendship dramas and school stresses by providing a safe harbour – the kitchen table I always imagined before they were born. Perhaps I've taught them something – I know they've taught me a lot.

Over twenty years of motherhood I've had time to make mistakes and learn from them. I've had time to absorb my own diagnosis and reassess my life experiences through the lens of autism. One day I'll be an autistic grandmother, I hope. I intend to be gloriously eccentric, with a garden full of plants and flowers, animals and birds, and a house full of books and craft things. I look forward to that.

Intersected Like Me

Mrs Kerima Çevik

Content note: Racism, ableism, bullying

The year I was born, a disabled veteran and journalist, who was later designated a reluctant Civil Rights Movement ally, published a book that told the story of his journey to understand Black people. John Howard Griffin had studied Black people, and believed he sympathised with their struggles for equality, but he did not understand them. What he did was nothing short of shocking. *Sepia*, a Black magazine, agreed to fund a social experiment in exchange for a series of articles on what happened to the white native of Dallas, Texas.* Then, he went to a doctor and had a series of treatments to make himself Black.

He spent the following weeks living and travelling as a Black man in the segregated South. When the journey was over, he believed he finally knew the full experience of being Black in a segregated world. This misplaced certainty defined the rest of Griffin's life. He spent most of his remaining years wrestling

---

* Griffin, John Howard. *Black Like Me.* Houghton Mifflin, 1961. LCCN 61005368.

with the belief of white society that because he had 'lived' as a Black man he therefore understood, from this limited experience, every aspect of the intersections of racism, classism, poverty and myriad other facets of being Black in America. He later came to realise that this belief harmed the people he meant to provide a better understanding of. As the Civil Rights Movement gained momentum and eloquent, strong, African American voices rose to the challenge of speaking truth to power, Griffin became increasingly uncomfortable being called upon to be the interpreter of Black voices and behaviour to white stakeholders in the social justice conversation.*

Griffin did learn some unique things in the South, including something he had failed to notice before: the way white people spoke to one another was different from the language they used to address Blacks. Communication between races itself was structured to remind Blacks that they were less than whites.

Griffin's advantage was that he could leave the oppressive world of being Black in segregated and racist America at will; those he left behind could not. Study and experimentation cannot replace the lived experience of oppression.

Just as Griffin's perspective on Blackness was necessarily contextual and limited, regardless of his temporary immersion and study, parents of neurodivergent children can also find

---

* Bruce Watson, 'Black Like Me, 50 Years Later', *Smithsonian Magazine*, October 2011, available at smithsonianmag.com/arts-culture/black-like-me-50-years-later-74543463

themselves caught in the gap between knowing and unknowing. The problem of experiencing discrimination is compounded when a parent is trying to be an ally to their neurodivergent child, precisely because unless that parent is also neurodivergent in exactly the same way, they cannot quite understand the endemic nature of ableism and how a combination of structural and disability-specific ableism impacts the quality of their children's lives.

For example, they may be unaware that they are perpetuating that ableism by using the language constructs of a society that endemically discriminates against anyone visibly different. Even parents who may discover later in life that they are neurodivergent carry a lifetime of toxic negative stereotypes about brains wired differently, and the cognitive dissonance created when said parent discovers the truth of their own neurology can be painful to watch. When we are in crisis, we fall back on what we know, even if what we know is both harmful and wrong. Parents are not always able to view learning of their own neurological differences as an opportunity to open a new world of thought about their offspring. Parents who aren't neurodivergent or those who can don the false identity of a non-autistic parent may at times be able leave the world of disability and ableism. Their non-speaking neurodivergent children cannot. And children grow up.

As a parent, I must be keenly aware of the differences between lived experience and understanding. In trying to facilitate life for our son, at first, I looked to where my own differences made me vulnerable to greater discrimination. I knew what racism was by direct experience; I knew what sexism was as well. I also knew prejudice against religion and national origin. What I didn't know was discrimination based on a person's diverse neurology, and how this compounded my son's vulnerability to maltreatment when combined with his race, his father's immigrant background, my race and origins, and anything else that made him visibly different.

Correspondence from our son's time at a state-funded school in the US revealed plainly where discrimination was taking place. A parent accused our son of attacking her child and other children on the bus because 'his father was a brown man from India', even though my husband is of Turkish descent and clearly white. Both the school and the transportation office of our school district informed the parent in question that our son could not have attacked any child because he had always been placed in a safety harness on the bus and was actually the victim of an assault by another student. Request forms for reduced-price lunches were repeatedly sent home with our son because his teaching team insisted that, since I was dark-skinned, I must be on welfare. My surname was incorrect in letters addressed to us because it was assumed that as I was Black, I was not married to my son's father. When our son returned to school after recovering from a disability-related illness, I wrote in his communication book

33

that I was sorry he missed the annual trip to the pumpkin patch. His teacher responded that it didn't matter because he was a non-verbal autistic, and non-verbal kids don't even know what's going on anyway because they are so (insert pejorative term for intellectually disabled here).

I cannot go to a doctor and ask her to give me treatments to make me appear more non-verbally autistic, and doing so would still make me a tourist. Passing is not equivalent to being, and passing as a non-verbal autistic is not equivalent to being a non-verbal autistic in a world that demands verbal communication. How then, could I understand ableism better? After homeschooling my son for about two years, I believed I had found the answer. To understand what my son was up against, I needed to do better than what John Howard Griffin had done.

I began writing to autistic adults around the world who either used Augmentative and Alternative Communication (AAC) in the form of speech devices to speak, or who did not use verbal speech until they were much older. People who knew what it was like to be my son. I began reading their books and blog posts. I asked them questions. I was amazed when they answered and gave me advice on how to help my son communicate without verbal speech and self-regulate in an ableist world.

Still, there was something missing. His race, his national origins, the rest of who he was and how that influenced his life was not being addressed. One of the only people in the world who might come remotely close to understanding how our son's differences intersect to impact his life experiences is his sister. His sister is multiracial and multicultural too, and only unlike her brother in that she is not male-presenting or a non-verbal autistic. Somehow I had to listen to his communications to me, hear his sister as she explained the experience of being the multiracial daughter of a mixed-race marriage, and listen to non-verbal autistic disability rights advocates of colour communicating the experience of being non-speaking and non-white in a world of verbal speech and white privilege.

It is not an ideal solution to understanding ableism in combination with racism and other bigotry. I cannot be my son. I can't travel the world for a year as a non-speaking neurodivergent person, then presume I know what a lifetime of being non-speaking, multiracial and autistic means. But I am doing the next best thing. I can listen and learn from everyone who can teach me what happens when multiple differences meet at that intersection of minorities that is our son. I can improve the quality of his life by that understanding, allowing him as much agency in his life as he can manage. He is gaining confidence and losing fear. I hope that, hand in hand, my son and I can arrive at that crossroads and meet the challenges of overcoming each aspect of discrimination he encounters. He continues to teach me to express joy and laughter without restraint, to be as he is. Unfettered and intersected like me.

Further suggested reading

Alisha Gaines, *Black for a Day: White Fantasies of Race and Empathy*, University of North Carolina Press, 2017.

Shapes in Dreams

Amelia Wells

Content note: Descriptions of being drunk

I am drifting down a river, in a boat. There are five of us. Five. I remember five. One, two, three, four, five. I dip my hand over the side and drink the—

Opening the first eye is always the hardest. I wake up to the 'Imperial March' from Star Wars and I can press the snooze button with my eyes closed. Sometimes I do it in my sleep. In films they always open both eyes at once, really wide, then spring up, gun loaded, ready to face the zombie invasion. Or sleepily crack an eye at the alarm clock, which shows a time later than the time they had professed they must get up by in a previous scene, with hilarious results. The second eye follows. I stare at my ceiling, one hand on my alarm clock, the cool curvature of Vader's helmet in my palm, and the other hand wrapping my blanket tighter around me, rough wool itching my fingers, burrowing deeper under the duvet which protects me from November air, creeping in through the chinks of closed windows.

Nothing is better than a cosy warm bed except a toasty hot shower. The thought of burning water pouring down my back, pounding my shoulders, inspires tropical fantasies. The bathroom is blank white and freezing. Spiders live in the light fittings, cobwebs gather around the bulb. Water hangs from the threads, washing line above a street. Knocks come at the door. The waterfall prevents me replying to the reminder that we are not made of hot water. Human beings are 60 per cent liquid and have a core temperature of thirty-seven degrees. Shampoo dribbles in my eye.

We are paddling upriver, our boat rocking from side to side with the motion of our oars. I remember oars. One each, dip and pull over one side, dip and pull over the other. We move, left to right, forwards. Splinters protrude from the rough wooden handles, work their way into my hands, nestle under that first layer of skin. Water pours from the oars, chases the space left in the river by me, dipping and pulling, over and over. My shoulders burn, over and over. Warm sweat dribbles down my forehead. We are struggling towards up. Rivers flow from mountains to seas. We are anti-flow, from seas to mountains. Maybe we have come from the sea. Maybe we live in the mountains. I rest my oars and dip my hand over the side. Water rushes into my cupped palm. I pull the miniature pool towards my mouth and drink the—

Coco Pops versus Weetabix. Two boxes stand to attention. The empty bowl waits in front of me, a ring of light nestling at the bottom. Gaping maw, ready to be filled. I drown the light with milk. Coco Pops make the milk go chocolatey, the cheery monkey says so, but they have to sacrifice their crisp coco-ness for this phenomenon to occur, leaving a bowl of brown milk filled with floating dirty-white ex-rice pieces swirling away from the spoon.

Weetabix absorbs milk completely, a cereal sponge. The pink flowered tin marked 'Sugar' contains raisins. I pick the bowl up, tip it towards my mouth, drain the milk out, gulps interspersed with handfuls of Coco Pops, straight from the box, no mixer. The bowl joins the others, balanced on a pile already three high, leaning towards the sink. I tuck the plastic bag back into the cardboard box, folding it to keep it airtight, tuck the jutting cardboard flap into its corresponding slit. Coco Pops before Weetabix, both in front of Shreddies. They line up in the right-hand cupboard, next to tins of new potatoes and dark-chocolate digestives. I place the bowl stack on the plate stack and push them against the wall. The steam hasn't yet dispersed from the bathroom. Some finger has traced 'wash up' in the condensation on the mirror. I brush my teeth, grab my coat and go.

The other four sit, two to a bench, one oar each, dipping and pulling, pushing us faster down the river – I let my mind wander out of the boat and rest my eyes on the surface. Bubbles hustle past, hurrying to be downriver. My fingers trail the boundary between air and water, breaking the skin, leaving their own ripples and eddies in the clear water. The riverbed rises to my fingertips, mud and grit carried away by the current, turning the clear water brown. Rushes sway lackadaisically up from the riverbed, brown and green lengths undulating from one side to the other, over and over, slowly, calmly; just beneath the surface. The reeds have nowhere to go and all the time to get there in. They point us down the river, towards the sea. My fingers brush the rushes, slip along their slimy surface and the boat rushes on, oars dipping over one side, then the other, over and over. I pull my fingers away from the weeds, water dripping from my fingertips onto the boat. I raise my fingers towards my face, letting the water drip from my fingertips into my—

Someone told me once about the garden on the roof of the library. I stand outside the glass doors, shielding my rolly from the wind. The game is to keep it lit. Inhale long and hard, 'til the end glows orange past the tip of your nose. Exhale and watch the smoke curl up away into the sky, past all four floors of the grey building. Even non-smokers have clouds on their lips. Sparrows perch on the wires criss-crossing the roof. No substitute for branches. I live on the second floor, between Juvenal and Dickens. Soft breathing turns pages down the aisles. Talking is not permitted, except in the group-study areas. I sit cross-legged in the stacks, slide my fingers between the books, PD4583, PD4588, turning to indexes, searching for the words 'social ills'. Thick yellow leaves flick between my fingers; fact opinion fact opinion. Someone told me once that Bible pages make good rolling papers; that they had chapters of Corinthians in their lungs.

The Romantic Self lies open to page 264. I place a Rizla in the centre crease. My bag lies open to the side of me. I reach inside for my wallet and remove a return ticket, tear away an orange strip and curl it up. The roach sits in the Rizla. I reach for my tobacco, grazing my fingers on the rough green carpet, lifting my hips to slide the pouch from my back pocket. The tangle of baccy knots from 'country' to 'house'. My fingers feel through the pouch, pushing the tobacco close, pulling it apart. Hash is harder than tobacco, even good squidge. I feel the tiny disc, all I have left, extract it, press my palms together around it, softening it. My fingers smell like flowers. I roll it into several cylinders, nestle the hard brown hash into the enveloping soft brown baccy at 'country', 'not', 'time', 'fallen', 'house'. I pick the paper up, push my fingers up, pull my thumbs down until the leaf encircles the roach, baccy, hash. Lick it, stick it, tuck it up my sleeve. A book falls down from the shelf above me, misses my head. Words of apology tumble down after.

41

The river forces the boat on and my knuckles turn as white as the rapids from gripping the side. The water rages around us, swirling in front and behind, stretching on in front and behind, straight. Grey rocks break the water near the bank; the river rushes between them. Spray flies up, falls like rain onto the boat. Sunlight catches in the spray, refracts into red, orange, yellow, green, blue, indigo, violet. Richard of York gave battle in vain. Rainbows drip down my neck, stick my T-shirt to my back. We are moved towards blue sky above us by brown water beneath us, straight on, in the middle of the river. Clouds flit past in the water, hovering just below the surface, quick silver fish not altering their path to avoid them. I expect to see fish in the sky, the river reflecting the sky, reflecting the river. Oars clatter against each other in the stern; we could not influence the boat any more than we could stop the river by standing and commanding it. The other four are huddled together in the middle of the boat. The middle of the boat in the middle of the river. I wonder if we are in the middle of the sky. The enormous, infinite sky, stretching further to each side than I can see, everywhere and nowhere, stopping only because the horizon interrupts it. Dull green and brown trees mar the deep blue sky; branches reach towards the clouds, seeking to bring them back to the earth. When we see sky, we see light particles refracting through the atmosphere to create blue. I know this. I cannot remember my own name. I do not know who these people in the boat with me are. They huddle together in the middle of the boat, in the middle of the river, beneath the centre of the sky and I recognise their faces. They are faces, with two eyes each, a nose, a mouth, hair and ears. I recognise their faces. I push my fingers between the clouds and draw them out, glistening, dripping. I let the wet drip into my—

Ink splatters across my notes. The last few sentences rendered illegible by rain, which stains. I copy it from the board a second time. Black puddles sink into white paper. Desks are arranged in a square formation to promote debate. The old classroom style, with the teacher at the front, is deemed too formal. I watch the clock, waiting for the big hand to complete its circuit above the lecturer's head. She draws a mushroom, marks eyes and mouth on it. I paddle my fingers in the pools, push my forefinger into the top right corner. Whorls and ridges smudge above the poem, full of soft sounds, creeping up on the ear.

Sunlight drifts in the window, illuminating dust particles, dancing. Five fingers and four corners makes twenty. Four fingers and one thumb. I push my thumb down above the mark made by my forefinger. Repeat. Add in eyes and mouths with my pen. A mushroom army stands guard of the poem. Ink seeps through the paper, making blotches on the pale blue table. Patterns swirl out like shapes in dreams, a rabbit with a crooked ear, an apple, a telegraph pole. We're above scrawling our names on desks now, the graffiti of academic boredom. I wipe my pen with a tissue, watch the ink flowering across it. I crumple the tissue around the nib, pull it away, put it in my pocket.

Black coffee seeps out across the tabletop towards my elbow, emphasising the slow, steady march of the mushrooms towards our civilisation, threatening to soak up all my words. It unfurls towards me, scalloped edges, and I push my chair back as it spills over, flows down the table leg. The word 'bacon' stands out in white beneath the cascade, the steady rhythm of syllables build up the ominous nature. Other chairs scrape across the tiled floor, arms are shoved into coats. I shut my folder, click the lid onto my pen, wind my scarf around my neck.

I am grasping two oars and pulling them back, lifting them, pushing them forward, dipping them and pulling them back, over and over, slowly, steadily. I don't know where I am going. Rough wood makes its imprints on my hands. Maybe the skin on my palms used to be soft. Now it is creased, calloused. I can't see where I am going. There isn't a lot I can see. The riverbanks are shady and vague. Grey fog glides across the oily surface of the water. Mist writhes around the reeds, which sway gently, pulled back and forth by the eddies and undulations. Grey-green trees grow out of the darkness, branches hang across the river, crooked and black. I breathe in water from the air, the riverbanks fade a little more into darkness. A vine trails into the boat, slithers over my shoulder and slides out. A drop of water trails down my cheek, glides along my jaw. I slip my tongue out to catch—

Table Five is leaving as I arrive; thick coats rub past each other in the doorway. Clean white aprons hang off the clothes horse. The other evening shift pulls hers tight, knots it, slides an order pad and pen into the pocket and pushes past me before I can unzip my coat and swing my bag over my head. I find a pen, make a mark halfway down my order pad. Top section for drinks, bottom section for food. Golden lights glance off the wet cobblestones outside, highlighting the darkness. The door swings open, the couple bundle in, are shown to Table Five. I scrape food from one plate to the other; peas roll down the ceramic slope into mashed potato hills. Rain drips from their coats onto the stone floor. Half-empty glasses to the bar, gravied plates to the kitchen. Table Five browse the menu, pausing at the starters, perusing the drinks. I wipe away crumbs, place napkins and cutlery parallel to the table edge. The knife reflects an oak beam, chipped plaster. He orders the house red, two glasses; she asks for white, and the fish. A spoon clatters to the floor. Salt smells stream down the stairs. Table Eight would like some clean cutlery. He considers the fish. I point out the Specials board; green chalk leaves curl in its corners. Table Ten would like some water. Tap water. A jug. Please. I push the corkscrew into the cork, twist it deeper, pull down the silver arms until the cork pops out. The soup of the day is leek and potato. He decides on the fish. Another bread roll. Steak is served with a blue cheese or peppercorn sauce. Soup slops onto the saucer. Table Two just want the bill. I place the leather wallet holding the addition of their meal next to the half-sponge pudding, ruined castle with a moat of cream. The fish eyeballs me, mouth mid-sentence. Ketchup is squeezed from its plastic container into a ceramic dish to look more presentable. I wipe away crumbs, bomb the castle with ice-cream napalm, bowls to the kitchen. More red. Another glass. Two more seated at Table Six. The desserts menu. Please. I keep the change. Blood trickles from the steak. Cutlery placed parallel to the napkin, napkin placed parallel to the edge. Thank you. One chocolate brownie, one fruit crumble. None of our main meals contain nuts. Cream, custard or ice cream?

Someone waves at me from the bank. I have given up rowing; the oars chafe. We are heading downstream anyway, no particular destination, none that we know. I vote we let the river take us. The river knows more than we do, flows from the mountain to the sea. Maybe we will reach the sea soon. A figure motions towards me from behind a clump of bulrushes. I see a glimpse of dark red hair and the boat has moved on. I remember dark red hair. Inside me in a dark room is a small voice. It shouts about dark red hair. I lock the door on its dark room. In the boat, dark red hair turns towards me and offers me an oar. I want to tell them there's no point in rowing. We won't get to where we don't know we're going any faster. What will we do differently when we reach the sea? If we reach the sea. If there is a sea to be reached. My mouth doesn't open; my fingers clasp around the rough wooden handle. Flakes of white paint stick to my palm. Once this boat was white. Maybe this boat had a name once. Maybe I had a name once. I push the oar into the water and let it go. Someone waits for it on the shore. They lift it in salute and disappear into the trees. Dark red hair turns to me, wrinkles crease in their forehead, a disappointed frown. I dip my hand over the side, cup the water into my palm. White flakes drift in the palm pool. I tip my head back and pour the water down my—

I push open the door, immediately overheat in the crush of bodies. *Slainte*. The crowd refuses to make any concession to my existence. Laughter rolls over my head, warm beer breath rolls into my ear. Burberry scarf moves an inch. I duck under Guinness and spot her, table in the corner beneath the black and white, wrinkled, grinning man, chicken tucked under the crook of his arm. A pint of Strongbow sits by the empty stool. I run my thumb down the side, turn the glass, run my thumb down the side until all the condensation is gone. He's like a bacon sandwich someone offered before realising they didn't have any bacon. Or bread. She waves her glass of rosé in front of her frown. A single drop clings to the rim. On the windowsill the flame flickers twice on the thick squat candle, twice again in the reflection, and her eyes flick behind me to the door. A cat jumps onto the wheelie bin, climbs vertically up the fence. I push salt around the tabletop, in and out of deep crevasses. Shepherding it with inky fingers into a smiley face, a balloon, the Eiffel Tower. She blows across my shapes; salt scatters like stars. Another glass, another pint. He's a toy in a shop that she can visit but never buy. Its not that she can't afford him, more that he doesn't want to be afforded. She upends the bottle; dregs trickle into her glass as her metaphor drains away. He won't get out of the box. She can't get him out of the box. He has a 'try me' button, but he won't be bought. She pats the bottom of the bottle, places it carefully not quite on the table, ignoring the thud, heading for the toilet door, catching her fingers on the outside of the doorframe to swing herself through. I pick up the bottle, place it in a dark knot of just the right size.

They have games around the corner. Games and a couple of spare stools. Dark eyes stand next to her. Eyes crinkled at the edges, hand pushes hair out of dark, crinkled eyes. We know there are games around the corner; we come here every week. Connect Four and Articulate stack on a wooden bookcase by the miniature plough. The game is out. Boxes give out triple word scores. I straddle the spare stool, reaching into the green bag. A.F.G.H.Z.Q.I. Another pint, another bottle. Rough. She tugs at her fringe, no longer wanting a bacon sandwich. Horse. Sharp bubbles race down my throat. Quiz. T.O.S. I look up into dark, crinkled eyes. Shame. No one is taking score. They decide to crown the winner based on the most interesting word. Mats. Narrative builds up on the board. Wit. They exchange words at speed. I exchange letters. F.H.T. for O.P.E. Wolf. She sips her wine, blinks quickly at the toy out of its box. Four. I fold the board, the rough wolf chases the witty horse back into the green bag. The candle on the table flickers, her eyes never leave his face.

The banks are too far away to be seen. We are still pulled by the current, but the boat bobs gently, down and up. I lie down the middle with the oars, wooden joists pressing into my spine, curving my stomach outwards. The deep blue sky spreads over me, stopped by the sides of the boat. Splinters push through my T-shirt, bury themselves in my skin. I can't see where we are going. Forwards. Down. Through a forest. Leaves appear in the sky, at the edges. Green spears pointing upwards. Pointing out into space. Behind the deep blue is deep black. Behind the deep blue is dark night. The sun shines down, water sprays up the side, arcing over the boat. Completely clear. Blue, because the sky is blue. Transparent. Even water has a shadow. I reach up, turn my hand around in the spray. Droplets trickle down my arm. The others watch me, look at the river, watch me. Water spills in over the side. I open my mouth to catch the—

Red. Yellow. Blue. White black white black. Bodies writhe and crush together, skin turning green, purple, red, yellow, orange. Heavy beats pass through hip bones, high-pitched vocals wash over the mass of movement. I stand at the bar, someone's sweaty, hairy arm pushed against mine, their shoulder pressing into my nose. Pints are placed to the right of me, and shot glasses filled with advocaat, grenadine, Midori. Red sinks through green; Squashed Frogs disappear down throats, tossed back, and hairy arm collects the pints, removes his shoulder from my face. My skin peels away from the surface of the bar. Cider. Pint. Rosé. Bottle. My hands shape the glass sizes, point to the tap. Drum and bass emanates from moving lips. Ten outstretched fingers, five outstretched fingers, one bent index finger. Change comes in pound coins and silver shrapnel. Cold circles in my palm. I push them into my pocket, tuck the chilled bottle into the crook of my arm, pick up the pint and glass. Condensation runs down my forearm.

I put the glasses down on the table in the corner. She sits, legs curled across his thighs, one shoeless foot hooked behind his knee. Her hair covers both their faces. They move through blue light, hands parting hair, stroking cheekbones, pulling earlobes. I pull out my baccy and Rizla. The wind fights to put out my cigarette. I cup my hand around it, lean on the rough brick wall. Starlight turns the green trees grey. Smoke rises into my nostrils. I turn on the tap, soak my hands beneath the gushing water, turn my wrists to cool them in the stream. The smell of vomit catches in my throat. My eyes are rimmed red, bloodshot. I wipe my hands dry. Vodka spills across the bar. A slice of lemon, a pot of salt. Lick, down, suck, wince. I take my pint. Cigarette leans forward, unlit. Lamp posts turn the grey concrete orange. I flick my Zippo open, fire flickers upwards. The tip glows, breath drawn in, smoke exhales. His fingers pull at her hair, her hands grip his neck. My hands shape the glass sizes. I push through the crush, part writhing bodies. Cider spills, sticky down the side of the glass. I close my eyes, see white shapes moving on the insides of my eyelids. Red. Yellow. Green. White. Black. White. Black.

I am drifting down the river in a boat. There are five of us. Five. I remember five. One, two, three, four, five. The boat is quite small and made of wood. Oars clatter in the stern, rolling from side to side with the motion of the water. The river is wide and currents pull us, push us, forwards and sideways. There is no rudder, it is a rowboat, but we stay in the middle of the river, rocking slightly. The other four sit in the middle of the boat; I sit near the prow, looking forwards, looking towards the end of the river. The mouth that opens into the sea. On each side, the riverbank passes by, trees looming over patches of bulrushes through which fish flit. Behind me, the four huddle. Above me, the sky stretches up out and forever. Beneath me, the boat rocks from side to side, splinters dig into my knees. I remember five. I remember words. I trail my fingers between the boundary of air and water. I cup my hand and pull my own pool from the river. White flecks of paint float in my palm. I draw the water towards my mouth and drink.

My room seems a little softer at the edges. I stumble into the edge of my desk. This blurriness is in my eyes, not the physical structure of the world. I switch the light on, the window becomes a mirror. I stand in front of hills and fields, transparent. Straight hedges mark out square fields to keep in sheep and cows. Sometimes they eat the hedges. I turn the light off. There are other lit rooms, most with the blinds down. Light creeps around the edges, lives just out of reach. People pulling off jumpers and putting on pyjamas. People lighting incense and writing diaries. People going over their to-do lists and brushing their teeth. People removing other people's jumpers and not putting on pyjamas.

I pull the cord and the blind drops onto the windowsill, dislodging a photo frame. I drop my jeans, grab at my bed in the dark for my T-shirt. I fumble through my pockets, dislodge my lighter. The glow is the only light in the room. I inhale harder, it glows brighter. I tap the ash off into the ashtray, turn out the light.

Untitled and Tension

Tjallien de Witte

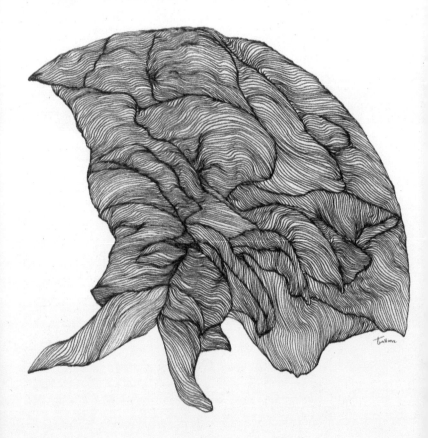

Untitled and Tension

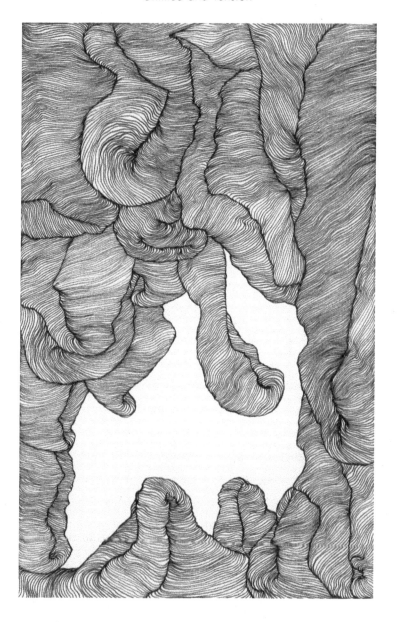

This Love

Nell Brown

When I was twenty-nine, I got a diagnosis of autism spectrum disorder. It took a little while to be assessed – a couple of fevered and stressed years – and, at thirty-one, I'm still not sure what to do with this diagnosis, how it maps onto me. It can feel like a revealed number that balances out an equation; it can feel like a template stuck onto and obscuring me.

Waiting for my assessment, I got stuck on the idea of 'special interests'. This name, which I find slightly condescending, reflected the tone of the representations I knew from books, TV and films. An autistic special interest was the centre of a character's world, unchanging and singular; there wasn't space for much else. Showing how an interest manifested – how it obstructed social relationships and disrupted the lives of those around the autistic person – was more common than any exploration of the experience of being interested in something. It all seemed so simple: a special interest was obvious to everyone, concerned solely with fact-finding and communicated with insistence but – mostly – without joy. I felt like I was trying to understand myself in translation, holding up characters (most likely written by non-autistic people) to see how I compared.

Outside of fiction there was the Autism-Spectrum Quotient, a questionnaire developed by Simon Baron-Cohen that GPs sometimes use as a screening tool – I was referred to autism specialists based on my answers to it. I was struck by the focus on particular subjects or ways of spending time: I had to say if I was fascinated by dates and numbers; if I would rather go to a theatre or museum, to a party or a library. All of this led me to believe that some topics were inherently autistic and others were not, and I wasn't taken with that much in the autistic camp: maths, trains, *Star Trek*, dinosaurs, *The Lord of the Rings*.

In my late twenties, another surprise alongside the autism diagnosis: a fierce fascination with Taylor Swift. It grew slowly, or – maybe more accurately – waxed and waned over the years, before expanding massively. On reflection I can trace a string of loves going back to before I could even string together a complex sentence: Freddie Mercury, John Lennon, Kurt Cobain, Zack de la Rocha. Their music was a core part of each devotion, and with each era there was a different way of listening: a VHS of Queen videos that I watched on repeat as a toddler; a cassette of Nirvana songs I played until tape degradation warped and slowed the sound; the end-of-year notification from Spotify that I'd listened to Taylor for over ten days in total. Not for me the thrill of the new; instead, the thrill of hearing an anticipated melody, of an album unfolding the same way twice, three times, a hundred times. The pleasure of this isn't about being comfortable, though it can be a comfort. An album or song I've listened to thousands of times can still feel exhilarating – like falling for someone, your heart swelling and blooming in your chest like a flower, your blood rising and rushing in response.

A number of these obsessions stretched far beyond the songs – far beyond reality, even. When I was younger, my internal world was filled with cinematic fantasies of friendships with my icons. It didn't matter if they were dead: in my imagination I had a time machine, or I would wallpaper myself over someone with an actual connection to the musician (Tobi Vail, Sean Lennon). I gleaned details about a musician's life and interests from the songs they covered, from interviews and articles and books, giving my imaginings more texture and giving me new topics to learn about. These fantasies took my time and concentration, but I didn't talk about them. I didn't feel the need to share them and also didn't want to have something precious to me interrogated or mocked – I knew my taste wasn't aligned with that of my classmates when, aged about seven, I argued that the Beatles were better than Take That. Sharing the worlds I created would open them up to others, risking unexpected disruptions, similar to the way my older sister had once described, in great detail and completely incorrectly, my childhood imaginary friend.

Pop music is sensory and emotional and intellectual all at once. I can let myself be overwhelmed by someone else's emotions and life, or get lost in layers of meaning, picking apart and analysing lyrics, researching and puzzling over references (Nirvana, for instance, taught me that the leaves of the pennyroyal plant were historically used as an abortifacient). Anchored by one figure, an interest can expand sideways (these days I'm fascinated by fandom and celebrity brand building, and by bearding, when staged heterosexual relationships are used to hide someone's true sexuality). And it's much easier now. I once carried round a pocket-sized fact book about Freddie Mercury, but today, if my phone is on, I can find the answer to a question as soon as it pops into my mind, much to the detriment of my sleep cycle. Devoted fans analyse Taylor's every move, encouraged by the singer's self-confessed tendency to litter her interviews, songs and videos with clues about future releases or song meanings. I've found podcasts that break down the production of a song (ideal, as I have neither musical education nor talent) or explore queer themes in Taylor's work.

Sometimes I feel overwhelmed by my curiosity – compelled, ravenous. This sounds more negative than I mean it to. It can be disruptive and tiring: I've had days at the office spent not doing work, taken by a new subject and too curious to care that I'm very obviously watching videos about it on YouTube; I've spent the early hours awake and reading, even though I'm bone-tired and know I should sleep. But it can also feel wonderful, an electricity your body can't quite contain, your brain entirely absorbed and racing whippet-fast to keep up. Sometimes it's slower: a subject grabs and holds your attention for a moment, then months later you realise it takes up a significant space in your brain and you didn't notice it happen.

Over the years, I've shifted perspective, reframed special interests as something akin to a relationship with a person. (This analogy can be tricky if your interests involve real people, so let me be clear: it *is* an analogy.) Think of the quiet crush that fills the space between turning off the light and going to sleep, or an excited first love that colours your conversations and shapes your daydreams. Think of someone you cared for deeply but don't see any more, or a years-old friendship that is nourishing and stimulating and intense. Interests don't have to be a fixed point around which a life revolves, though like a new lover you can get drunk on them – giddy and eager to find out everything, unable to concentrate on your fucking work or the chores you have to do. Like an ex, you can resent them – know that they are taking up too much of your time, and that you'd like to think about something else now, please. You can outgrow them, as you can a person. You don't have to love something wholly or without complication, and its appeal can sometimes be grim: an interest can take root because a subject irritates or frustrates you (the plot of many a romcom).

This isn't a perfect analogy, of course, but thinking of interests in a similar light to relationships and friendships complicated what had been flattened or simplified in mainstream representations of autism. It gave me space to think about all the forms an interest could take and how it could be expressed or even kept secret; it gave me space to think about an emotional connection to interests, all the complexities of feeling that give such connections texture. And just as my relationships are shaped by personality, mood and needs, so might my interests be. Some autistic people might find joy in being like detectives, piecing together evidence, data, theories; I am more than happy to benefit from somebody else's hard work (though I might also believe I could have done it better if I'd wanted to, because I am arrogant as well as lazy).

My interest in Taylor Swift plays out in a different way to most of the others I've mentioned: I have easy access to a fandom that sprawls across time zones and social media sites, a network of people who want to talk about anything Taylor-related. Different communities spring up around particular perspectives or interests, and I've found myself fascinated by those who believe Swift isn't straight. A sense of there being a queer reality hidden by societal and industry homophobia inspires dedicated theorising, with fans collecting supposed signals and clues over the years that run counter to the public story.

Dipping my toes in, I wondered why being part of a community like this isn't an established autistic stereotype. Pop fandom is catnip for anyone with an eager and hungry interest. Aside from the music and music videos, the glamour of celebrity combined with current media culture equals a river of articles, interviews, pictures, news stories. The potential for deep exploration is there; for creativity, with fanfic; for collecting, if that's your thing – merchandise, vinyl, magazines, gigs; for socialising that doesn't judge excessive interest. This isn't to say I want pop fandom added to a certified list of 'intrinsically autistic interests'; if it isn't clear already, I don't think there are any. It is telling, though, that certain subjects and even fandoms have become synonymous with autism and others haven't, even when they – very obviously to me – share qualities.

I sometimes wonder if the 'extreme male brain' theory of autism, which was popular when I was growing up, plays a part in this. It is based on the idea that if you drew up a continuum of human behaviour ranging from 'empathetic' to 'systematising', women would be grouped at one end and men at the other, with autistic people appearing near the systematising 'male' end. A theory like this, coupled with wider societal investment in categorising different interests and behaviours as male or female, shapes people's expectations about what subjects autistic people should enjoy. The popular belief that we are robotic – unemotional or disconnected from humanity – is also important: how could any of us be intensely interested in a person, or part of a fandom that is commonly derided as having too much feeling?

I think back to those representations of autistic people I once reached for, and wonder if they explain why some people tell me that I don't seem autistic. I wonder how many people see such characters when they imagine autism; I wonder how many mistake some of their shared traits (including maleness and whiteness) as inherent to autism, rather than seeing them as a repetition and amplification of one possibility. I wonder about the relationship between cultural stereotypes and medical ones: who are doctors overlooking?

I don't want to be penned in by the perceptions of non-autistic people, or by representations that stop at the surface or tell the same story again and again. I want to reclaim space; I want to rest my weight against the boundaries set by others and push against them. Writing this is a push, making a little more room for myself and – I hope – others. Can you feel it?

Becoming Less

Robert Shepherd

Content note: Disordered eating, ableism,
mental illness

1

I remember the day I first learned how few of us could live in a
world without civilisation. I was fifteen at the time, listening to
my biology teacher talk about things that had nothing to do with
our exams. Without farming, he'd said, the number of people in
the UK would be unsettlingly low – fewer than in a small city,
more than in a large town. There would be about as many people
as seals, because we were more or less the same size. And I
remember feeling disconcerted by that, like I'd never thought of
a seal as the same kind of creature as me. And that was the start
of it, I suppose: the idea that our species might have something
in common, that we'd have something useful to say to each other.

2

I wasn't very good at being a teenager, as my family would often
tell me. People my age were supposed to sneak out and get drunk

at night, while I would stay in reading books about biology. 'You should be rebelling against your parents!' my mother used to say. I was always quick to point out how ironic that was.

I remember thinking that what I was doing was rebellion, in its way. At that time it felt like the whole world centred around what a young person should be – and what that was did not resemble me at all. Staying in meant I was choosing what someone my age could be, whatever I'd been told by other people. In that way, studying biology began to become a form of quiet rebellion.

3

In the part of Scotland where I'm from, people once thought all the creatures on the land had their counterpart in the sea – for example, the horse might be twinned with the seahorse, although it was probably more complicated than that. And like all the other creatures, we had our analogues: the seals, the people of the sea. That was why no one would eat a seal if they could avoid it, and it might have been why we told so many tales of them. They were us.

I told the selkie about that once. I remember she said we were flattering ourselves.

4

Evolution was what got me interested in biology. It wasn't so much the process that interested me, but the realisation of how much time had passed for the world. As a child I'd known in a dim way that the earth was billions of years old, but reading that made me feel it: for the first time, I knew in my bones how small the human world really was.

I used that idea as a shield, I now realise. That sense of smallness can make it easier to block the world out, to ignore the billions of lives and experiences you don't quite know what to do with. You don't fit in, but your species doesn't either, so you shelter in your ignorance and call it a kind of wisdom. So I lived that way for the rest of my teenage years, convincing myself it was an intelligent thing to do.

5

I'd been diagnosed with Asperger's syndrome at ten and undiagnosed at the same age. It was wrong to label children at that age, my family said, and wrong to condemn them. I grew up thinking of the things autism brought as obstacles to overcome: I should look people in the eyes, I should stop being so anxious, my interests should be more normal than they were. I was taught that I didn't have any kind of autism, and came to believe that any signs I did were in fact just personal failures. So it was in that frame of mind as a teenager that I thought I understood the reality of the world.

6

I don't remember what I thought when she told me she was a seal. I probably wasn't as disbelieving as I should have been. It was Freshers' Week at Edinburgh University, and I'd met so many people I didn't believe were real. Someone had gone to Eton; someone else turned out to be royalty. By the time I met her, being a seal would seem almost relatable.

She didn't look like a seal, of course; she looked like an eighteen-year-old woman. She wasn't obese or blotchy-skinned, unlike myself. She was thin and had black hair. She seemed perfectly normal. Selkies are very clever in that way. They know exactly how to pass as human beings, which at that point was a skill that I didn't share.

She did say something I remember: that seals think it's a terrible disguise. It's so, so funny that we're fooled, she said. I have a photo of her, and I still look at it sometimes. A part of me still believes I'd be able to see.

7

She said I wouldn't understand where she was from, or why she was here. A starfish wouldn't understand what a chair was, she said, or much about the concept of accountancy. There was a whole human world that was closed to them. Why should it be any different when humans tried to comprehend the world of seals? She tried to explain, as an illustration, but it all seemed like nonsense to me.

8

I had a bad first week at university. I went on to have a bad first month, then a bad first year. But all that was still to come. Within the first hour of being dropped off at halls I was so anxious I threw up on someone, their food and myself. When I went to the toilets to clean up, I walked into the women's ones by mistake, where someone just looked at me, covered in sick and an inappropriate gender. They didn't seem shocked, or even sad. They looked like they knew they were part of someone else's story, one that didn't have a happy ending.

9

There were other reasons I'd become so invested in evolution. As a child I'd been told that the world was selfish and brutal, and that this was inevitable, unchangeable. In time, I became guilty for feeling love and compassion, like Darwin might come knocking on my door to tell me how this was wrong. So I began reading obsessively to try and find a justification for myself. If I could find a scientist who said that I should exist, I might begin to believe that I actually did.

10

There's a story told by a famous evolutionary biologist about a time he went to a museum to see all the mammals in the world arranged by their relationship to each other. He was an experienced scientist; he knew that evolution isn't about one species being better than another. But he still found it unsettling to see how the chart was arranged – people somewhere in the middle, and the seal at the end as the most evolved mammal of all. No matter who we are and what we know, it can be hard to see the world in a different way. The difference between me and him was that I've never felt I belonged at the top.

11

If you don't have selective mutism, you might not know what it means. It's not a conscious choice that you make so that you don't speak. It's the feeling that the parts of your mind that handle speech *are suddenly no longer there*; you open your mouth to say something and can't even make a sound. The longer I spent in halls without any human friends, the more I felt mutism come, and eventually it was normal that I was unable to speak at all.

12

I had friends outside university who, like me, were not seals in disguise. This was before the financial crisis, when the world seemed more hopeful than now, so a lot of us were doing subjects that didn't lead anywhere obvious, with the belief it would work out for us in the end. We'd always been told we were smart and we'd always succeeded at school, so we were very assured of the quality of our brains.

Looking back, it's hard for me not to draw a parallel between us and our species: always telling ourselves how very smart we were, to try and convince ourselves that we'd not made a horrible mistake.

The selkie was always putting our species down, pointing out stupid things we'd done. That might have been why we were friends, when I reflect on it. I've always had very low self-esteem.

13

She lived in a tiny flat with five other people, and I went there a few times, when I felt able. It was there she showed me her seal skin for the first time.

That's how they work, the selkies. When they want to come to the human world, they peel off their skin. Like all of them, hers was a full seal's skin, soft on the outside and slimy when turned round. Huge, thick and heavy, stuffed haphazardly in a wardrobe. She lit a lot of incense to disguise the smell.

(When I say she showed me her skin, you have to understand. It was because we were friends, because she trusted me. Not because of the other thing. The selkie stories of the place I'm from are full of that, of men forcing selkies to stay on land as their brides. They steal their skin and their lives, and I think they're supposed to be the heroes. In the stories a selkie is something less than a person, as a woman was, as a person still can be. I know it's not only me who gets angry when reading those stories. They are stories of violence against my friends, and stories of violence against me.)

I remember thinking that they took a part of themselves *away* to join our world. To live as humans do you cannot be everything you are; you disguise yourself by stripping bits away. It's how I think of myself now, when I think about how I behave; what I pretended to be and what I really am. My wardrobe stuffed with skin that I have shed; becoming normal; becoming human; becoming less.

14

A long time later when they trained my organisation around autism, they got an autistic person to explain what our worlds were like. It was done in the way that training like this usually is: to never say that neurotypical people see the world in the correct way, nor pretend a correct way could ever exist at all. But as the trainer says it I catch her eye, and I look, and we smile, and we know.

15

As autumn turned to winter, it all got worse. I came to accept that I would never make any more friends. In the halls where I lived, everyone ate together; I would sit alone and watch the smiling and laughing. The canteen was one of the few places to get food, but there were worse things than not eating. I began to shed something that wasn't skin.

When people talk about evolution, they say that 'the strong survive'. Weakness means death; that was the idea I'd wanted to challenge. If I learned more about evolution-as-science, then evolution-as-story might fall away; then I might feel able to be who I really was once again. Evolution is just about what will and won't survive, and survival doesn't care what people think is strong. But at that point in my life, as the snow fell down, the story felt more real than it ever had before.

16

Once or twice I walked through Edinburgh with the selkie, and neither of us would notice how it was beautiful. I would wince as an ambulance passed, its noise making me tense and my fingers twitch. She would growl at the asphalt on the road, muttering, *It's all the wrong shade of grey*. This world wasn't built for us, we knew. Every day there were a million reminders.

17

I had been told what first-years at university should do. They should be out clubbing and having sex; they should be ignoring all their lectures. They should be making friends and should be laughing. They should have little enough anxiety that they can leave their rooms. But my own first year was a world of not eating or washing, or ever properly managing to clean my clothes. My trousers became covered in washing powder that was stuck on; I smelled horrendous and got very thin. It never occured to me that someone might be able to help.

18

I did have some human friends in my first year, though, who believed the earth was only 6,000 years old. Evolutionary biology students meet a lot of people who believe the entire subject is a lie, who want to convince you that everything you think is wrong. It's the ultimate form of validation, to change someone's mind.

The first time I met them they said I would go to hell, and I was grateful for the warning. It would be cruel to think someone was damned for eternity and not even think to mention it to them. To them, evolution was something that it was necessary to destroy; an idea that implies goodness and morality can't exist. To me, it was the only thing that let me escape from a world that suffocated me, a reminder that a world exists that is less persecutory than the one people inhabit. We both created worlds to fit our own needs, and it was a matter of survival to believe it.

I asked the selkie about that, and she laughed. There was so much more than a human could know or see.

The other science students I met were very excited by facts. Increasingly I felt that I was not among them. I still believed science was the best explanation of the world we had. But something can be the best and can be inadequate as well.

19

I was sick every morning at that point; that's just what anxiety was. By the middle of the second semester I'd become too anxious to leave my room. We had a shared kitchen in halls that I was too shy to use, so I had to eat things that wouldn't grow rotten or spoil. I had a big box of oats that I'd mix with some chocolate paste, and eat them mixed together when I was able to eat anything at all.

We think of seals as fat, but they're not so bulky, really. A normal person has about as much fat in their body. But in the past us humans were much thinner, always living at the edge of starvation. And I was becoming someone who struggled to fit into my skin.

20

Eventually the selkie was the only person I spoke to, and even those conversations grew less and less frequent. I could tell that she was worried, which pleased me. It was nice that a seal could feel that way, or at least pretend to.

I never told anyone at the time, but I began to imagine going through my wardrobe, through all the clothes that smelled worse than the guts of a seal. I imagined searching until I found something that had always been there. An animal's skin is heavy and bulky, but the coat in my dreams was sleek – beautiful and silver like an invisibility cloak. I didn't think much about what happened after I put it on. I just knew when I did, I would be free.

A few weeks later, I found out she had gone; back to her home country, although no one seemed to quite know where that was. Somewhere in Europe, they said. I don't know why she left, or why she didn't mention it. I hope she knew I missed her, and what she'd meant.

21

For me, second year directly followed the first: a day after our final exams, we were in a field in the country to look at an odd kind of grass. I sat some distance from the other students, glowering at them as they all smiled and had a good time. For the first time, I realised that something might have gone deeply wrong.

I won't pretend that the story ended here. Recovering from how far I'd sunk took a very long time, and I had to unlearn a lot about what I thought was true of the world. But I began to meet other humans who had had experiences like my own, and started to identify with people who had never even thought of being seals.

I began to realise that what people thought could be normal let in more than I'd previously thought, and that human experience was wider than I'd known. It took me a long time to feel comfortable in my skin, and longer to be honest to others about who I was underneath it. But I wish my past friend and self had known how I was able to do both in the end.

22

I am much better now. Every time I am honest about my life, I expect it to be dismissed, and every time I find that I am wrong. I was never surprised I had a lot in common with seals. It took me a long time to realise the same was true of other humans.

It's now more obvious to the outside world that I am an autistic man. I'm stimming more, and finding sounds much harder. I've given up even pretending to make eye contact a lot of the time. But the effort of pretending is gone, and I'm free to do so much more. I have been liberated, and the value is hard to express.

I like to think the selkie left because she was bored. Anyone can pretend, just for a while. But eventually the sea calls and the tides swell; there is water to be felt on your skin. There is too much beautiful truth to spend so much time living a lie. And for that reason alone, I choose to believe she was happy.

The truth is that she wasn't exceptional, in the end. She had hidden depths I never knew; she felt things I'd never understand. It's only now I know that she was no different from any of us. She wasn't an enigma or a mystery. She was never a puzzle waiting to be solved. She was just an animal pretending to be a human, the same as all the rest of us in the world.

Escape to the Country

c. f. prior

Content note: Death, grief

We are an urban kind. Or so I'm told. Our stories take place in, between and beneath the metropolis. And if we're not already there we can't begin yet. Our lives are suspended until we relocate from nowhere to somewhere. Somewhere meaning New York, where David Wojnarowicz, with the river's winking chatoyant in his eyes, cruised the piers. Somewhere meaning San Francisco, where Sylvester sought refuge from the disapproving Pentecostal church in the company of a ragtag group of Black, queer, trans and cross-dressing folk called the Disquotays. Somewhere meaning London, where Yvonne Taylor and the rest of the Rebel Dykes could coalesce at thumping, hedonistic nights like Systematic and Chain Reactions. For those of us who weren't raised there, the city is a beacon, a bright symbol of escape, acceptance and the possibility that one might also find *somebody to love tonight.*

So many stories of queer life are mediated – even necessitated – by the city. But gender and sexual diversity are anything but anomalous outside the capital. Suburbs, coastlines and country lanes have all been sites of queer intimacy, affinity and kinship. For many, they've provided their own kind of imperfect refuge. As I began to reconsider my own relationship to the city and to my place in it as a queer trans person brought up between minute villages along England's south-east coast and the Oklahoma suburbs, I became drawn to stories of those who had made viable, interesting and even joyful lives away from the shadows of the city's skyscrapers. Places like Tove and Tuulikki's island at Klovharu, the comfortable, mirthful, unwatched freedom of Casa Susanna in the Catskills, and James Baldwin's house in Saint-Paul de Vence became for me a beacon signalling another kind of life, much like the teenage promise of London once did. They offered these people something the city couldn't, and I was keen to find out for myself what that was.

One might think of the suburbs, small towns, villages and the countryside as antithetical – if not actively hostile – to queerness. These spaces upon which the 'idea of a natural way of life: of peace, innocence, and simple virtue has gathered'* are not such simple spaces for queer folk. In contrast to the press, movement and crucial anonymity of the centre, these peripheral places punctuated here and there by a river's bend or by the raised index-finger of a church's spire, are, so the story goes, sad, lonely, and alienating places for queers.

---

* Raymond Williams, *The Country and the City*, Oxford University Press, 1975, p. 1.

In Sarah Waters' *Tipping the Velvet*, the protagonist Nan exchanges her sober life as an oyster shucker in Whitstable for a more bawdy one spent beneath lights on the stages of London's music halls. Miranda is ushered from a remote Maine Island crouched beneath a gauze of fog to the swell, vertical clarity of Manhattan in Aoibheann Sweeney's *Among Other Things, I've Taken Up Smoking*. It's only when, taken in by friends of her father's, a couple named Robert and Walter, that the fog concealing her own truths about herself and her desires is lifted. The countryside, we can conclude, is somewhere limiting, where queers stagnate or are prevented from flourishing. No wonder we all gravitate towards the proximity, intimacy and kinship of the city. Towards, as it were, the light.

When in my early twenties I moved first to Paris and then to London from an adolescence spent in Oklahoma, it was, in part, in pursuit of the same idea that drove Nan and Miranda towards the city. In those cities whose shared boundary was sheer possibility, I did feel better. Away from the watchful eye of the school administration, the piousness of the city, and my mother and stepfather, I felt free.* The physical distance, 4,634 miles to be precise, helped me establish psychic distance from a life in which I'd felt curtailed. In the city, life was different; I could embrace uncertainty, change, and play.

---

* The school which had on one occasion tried to expel me for wearing a T-shirt reading *Some Dudes Marry Dudes, Get Over It*, a punishment that was doled out, I assure you, to all students donning T-shirts with text on, and definitely not just the gay ones.

But more recently there were things that were beginning to unsettle me about the city. The arenas of desire I'd been so drawn to were closing at a pace. Astronomical rents had already driven out the gay bars, and now the queer club nights were being forced to capitulate too. Entire residencies were shorter than Ron Hardy sets at the Music Box. A few nights pulsed on, but even so, I worked long hours in draining administrative jobs for a pittance. I was caring for one of my fathers, Stephen, as his life came slowly to a close. I was too exhausted to party. I was too exhausted to cook. I was too exhausted to experience desire, let alone act on it. My relationship had ended and friends were all moving: Liverpool, Essex, Deal, Berlin. Places where the cost of living, financially and emotionally, seemed somewhat lower.

In 2017, Stephen died and as I was untethered by grief from situations that required courage, mettle and practical acumen, I began to question what exactly I *was* tethered to. It was a time of lassitude and relational fissures. It was a great unmooring. Drifting, questions began to gnaw at me. What if I moved? What if I returned to the sorts of places I'd once found so oppressive? Not what would I lose in moving away from the city's sprawl, but what might I gain?

I am certainly not the only one who has considered leaving the city. Every few years a spate of articles appears in popular publications enumerating the myriad virtues of The Big Move. In these articles, young, white heterosexual couples trade poky bedsits in London's Zone 2 for houses in happy Eden, leave office jobs to resurrect the honest work of brewing, farming, mom-and-pop shopkeeping and, of course, to get on the mythological property ladder. These articles are often written about folk who move through the world as smoothly as a reel of film passed through chamois leather – for whom suburbs, small towns and country pubs have never been anything but welcoming – and I'd already dismissed them wholesale.

Along with the ostensible promise of more space and time, a slower pace of life, being closer to Nature, the sentiment expressed in the articles is always accompanied by a shadow. Authentic, frictionless connections of life outside the city are pitched against the paucity or artificiality of interaction in an urban context. Not dissimilar to the way Hogarth* portrayed London in his print *Gin Lane,* these articles characterise the city as feverish, crime-ridden, and label ungentrified areas and, implicitly, their inhabitants, gritty. But what is cloaked beneath this disidentification with the city, and who gets to disavow it?

In a recent epitome of the genre, a heterosexual couple, in pursuit of that fabled community and more opportunities to climb or hike than either the Biscuit Factory climbing wall or

---

* Eighteenth-century cartoonist William Hogarth's print *Gin Lane* was designed to be viewed alongside, and in contrast to, another print called *Beer Street.* They represented a move away from satirical depictions of the faults of high society, towards satirical depictions of poverty and crime. They helped form the middle-class observer's opinion of Central London as a fetid and dangerous place.

the South Downs could offer, moved from London to the Lake District. With a loan and profits from the sale of their central London flat, they bought and became the custodians of a vast, dour Victorian hall. Built in 1860, it is situated in a valley whose name means 'pure' or 'clear'. Rooms at this Victorian guesthouse boast a Hackney-meets-the-Fells aesthetic. Mismatched furniture, of the kind that began to blight establishments around Brick Lane in the early noughties, peppers the rooms and hints at a kind of hackneyed, urban edginess made palatable for a monied clientele by its situation in a halcyon landscape. By importing the city's affects into an environment divested of any of the characteristics (and characters) that make a city a city, it becomes clear not just who owns the countryside, but who is welcome in it.

But life outside the city isn't simply a smooth, calm idyll anyway. It's not necessarily a sanitised, picturesque space. For a young Derek Jarman the countryside is, from his childhood Italian home at Villa Zuassa to his boarding school in Hordle, the location of eroticism, a geography of pleasure, those dazzling initial pulses of first love. What his first boyfriend, cocooned by violets, called 'the lovely feeling'.* No more is the countryside a limitless expanse inhabited by limited people than it is heterosexual. Or any one thing at all, for that matter; these are shifting, moving places, where the borders – especially

---

* Derek Jarman, *Modern Nature: The Journals of Derek Jarman*, 1992, p. 38.

at Dungeness – between sea, sky and shingle are blurred, as if smudged by a thumb. Shot through with classical and biblical references, the filmmaker's diary *Modern Nature* claims a corner of paradise for sexual dissidents, one that God forgot to document. And he intended to give it its due, to celebrate it in all its blurry, fluid, hedonistic glory. Where better to carve out space for queers in the garden, to rightly carouse in queers' honour, than amongst the sea thrift on the shale at Dungeness?

As a distraction from grief, I began to cruise the literature and art of the countryside, searching for its peripheral figures. And as is so often the case, once I'd uncovered one, more and more of these interlopers who defied common ideas about the countryside revealed themselves to me. I read about the long, queer history of rave and its presence in the countrside. I read about Rachel Carson and Dorothy Freeman, the Ladies of Llangollen and T. H. White. I attended events to hear about the queer inhabitants of places like Hebden Bridge, Province-town, and Appalachia. I scrolled endlessly through iO Tillett Wright's Instagram, filling my eyes with the California desert and filling my mind with plans.

Huddled under the covers on an icy Norfolk evening, I read about Derek Jarman's wild sea of kale, red valerian and foxgloves poking up at Prospect Cottage. Visiting a Barbican exhibition for my best friend's birthday, I learned about Casa Susanna, a resort in upstate New York where cisgender men and trans women could explore their gender presentation, play with and play out their gender fluidity and live, for a time, unbridled by expectation.

I noticed that artist Tove Jansson's work, from *The Moomins* to *Fair Play*, was chock-full of maritime paraphernalia, wide vistas and storms with thunder loud as cannon fire rolling in on the waves. I read her letters and found out that, having long dreamed of becoming a lighthouse keeper, she found not a lighthouse but an island on which she and her partner Tuulikki Pietilä could assemble hearths, make furniture, write poetry, attend to correspondence and read books about the sea, psychology and history. She described island life as 'a dream come true'.[*]

But the countryside doesn't only appeal to those who've known all their lives, like Tove, that they'd flourish in expanse, or to those who are returning to an old and familiar landscape, like Jarman. I recalled that in 1936 artist Claude Cahun, suffering from twin lethargy and political frustration, wanted to leave Paris. Growing anti-Semitism raised safety concerns for their life as part of a visibly queer Jewish couple, too. Cahun referred to the need to live in the countryside as 'a physical and primordial one' and once their partner Marcel Moore's mother died, they relocated to Jersey.[†] Despite Moore's initial reservations, the years before the Nazi invasion seemed blissful, peaceful. In a photograph from this time, Cahun, eyes

---

* Tove Jansson, *Letters from Tove*, 2019, p. 447.

† Jennifer Laurie Shaw, *Exist Otherwise: The Life and Works of Claude Cahun*, 2017, p. 199.

closed and mouth slightly open as if dozing, is surrounded by a halo of marram grass and irises in bloom.

Likewise, in 1971, after an adulthood spent in London, Paris and Istanbul, James Baldwin spent the last years of his life in Saint-Paul de Vence. What did a remote house on the edge of one of the French Riviera's oldest medieval towns offer this man doubly othered by his race and sexuality? He left the US for Europe aged twenty-four in a spirit of political opposition, but why would a writer whose work was so firmly situated in and so quintessentially *of* the city leave London, Paris, Istanbul?

It wasn't the first time. Years before he moved to the Alpes-Maritimes, he tried to set up home with a partner in a typical rustic stone dwelling with a galley kitchen and a slow wood burning stove in the Swiss municipality of Loèche-les-Bains. He moved to Chez Baldwin, his house in Saint-Paul de Vence, for the same reasons he'd moved to Switzerland: the city became a distraction, he couldn't write, he was beginning to wilt artistically. He needed to slow down, to establish a nurturing routine. It was peaceful, sure – sloping, snow-capped mountains juddered and then dipped into deep, glittering waters – but it was anything but soporific. Guests to the house included Josephine Baker, Nina Simone, Toni Morrison and Maya Angelou. Parties began late and ended early in the morning. Lovers bathed in dappled garden light came in and out of focus. In his house and the town he had found a safe and tranquil arena to recuperate but also a space of familial and homo-sociability he'd always desired. In his final inter-view, given at the house, Baldwin, resisting narrow readings of both his work and life, said, 'I was only fighting for safety, or for money at first. Then I fought to make you look at me.'* Chez Baldwin allowed him to make that final demand to be seen. Having been convinced that his exile from his homeland would make a perpetual nomad of him, he moved away from the city towards the town not to absent himself from the world but to find a settled space in it.

Like coming out, like childhoods of shame, isolation or bully-ing, migration to the city is considered essential to the queer mythos, a kernel at its very centre. It has been argued, time and again, that urban environments are better for queers, that they provide a level of anonymity coupled with sexual freedom that the claustrophobic ignorance of life outside the city simply can't. But just as I resist that coming out and shame are integral elements of queerness, or that there is only ever one universal story of queerness, so too do I resist the general assumption that the only queer lives lived outside the city are sequestered ones.

In the introduction to a discussion held at Tate Britain in honour of the filmmaker, painter and gardener Derek Jarman, the Tate director Maria Balshaw recounted a familiar tale of queer migration. In the story, Balshaw and friends – around

---

* Magdalena J. Zaborowska, *Me and My House: James Baldwin's Last Decade in France*, 2018, p. 116.

eighteen years old and seeking stimulation in the monotony of a small Midlands town – turned, as so many do, to the cinema. At a film house these friends saw Jarman's *The Last of England*, which was made in the wake of *Caravaggio* and his recent AIDS diagnosis; made too in the midst of a Thatcherite society marred by violence and homophobia. Upon seeing this film, with its themes of change and escape, one of her friends ran away from his family home to a new life in London, where he could come out, live and work as a gay man. Be free. But what about those who did it in reverse, what about those who never left or went back?

Jarman was one of them himself, of course. As the filmmaker was wrapping up *Caravaggio,* he inherited some money from his father. With it, he bought the house, 'its timbers black with pitch', on the shingle at Dungeness.* In *Modern Nature,* the volume of his journals published in the infancy of his time at Prospect Cottage, Jarman laments the incessance of the city. 'Would I write? Judge? Give advice? Attend? Approve? Help?' he asks.† Where London was a cacophony, it was also a reminder of the change he had undergone as a result of his diagnosis. No. He was happiest at home where he could, from his window, see the sea's deep azure, new

---

* Derek Jarman, *Modern Nature: The Journals of Derek Jarman,* 1992, p. 3.

† Ibid., p. 17.

growth sprouting on the clumps of lavender, the first drowsy bumblebee of the planting season.

There is a bit in a book I return to often about how the narratives we provide to make ourselves legible, as much to ourselves as to others, are unravelled by grief. One can try to plan for loss and one can set about to cope with it through any number of activities – God knows I did – only to find them useless. Much to my chagrin dancing, running, sourdough baking and gardening are not prophylactics for loss and are not enough to prevent being assailed by a stranger's resemblance, a scent, a particular turn of phrase or intonation. Something bigger is at play and it has other, often conflicting, plans for you.

Cut loose by loss, the bereaved have to remake themselves in the absence of their loved one and the absence of an imagined or desired future in which that loved one figures. It can be hard, horrible work. And there's no map. But in its own strange and unexpected way it can be clarifying too. This essay, which started as a distraction, became a cartography of queer lives, queer desires, and queer possibilities – and it showed me the way to another kind of future.

I have developed over this last year a habit of pilfering seed heads from the new planting scheme in my local park and from most floriferous front yards in my neighbourhood.* Some of these seeds have already become flowers and some of them

---

* I like to think that this practice follows in the footsteps of St Derek of Dungeness.

are squirrelled away for next year. As I submit this piece to my editor, the seed heads I've left untouched on my balcony garden are beginning to split open and spill next year's growth into the soil. Those that haven't have been harvested and shipped to my surrogate family in rural Wales and to a school friend's house in the desert outside Santa Fe. As they poke up their heads in their new homes, I too hope to be somewhere else, living another kind of life, not to run away from grief, but towards what it revealed to me.

It Has Nothing to Do with How I Look

Megan Rhiannon

it has nothing to do
with how i look

being autistic is not being able to shop
for groceries alone without becoming overwhelmed
by all of the options, sounds, sights and smells

it's having prepared mental scripts for social
situations and getting very lost very quickly
when the conversation deviates, resulting in a
lifetime of misunderstandings

and it's often becoming confused, overloaded and disoriented while alone and vulnerable in public, without being able to find somewhere safe and quiet to decompress

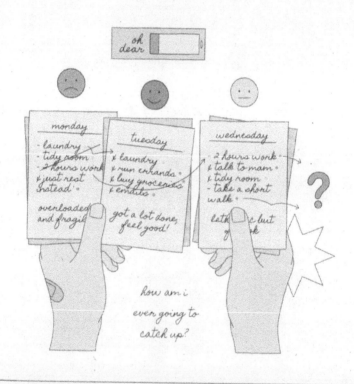

being autistic is having unpredictable and often fluctuating energy levels and abilities, and the consequences and setbacks that come with pushing yourself too hard

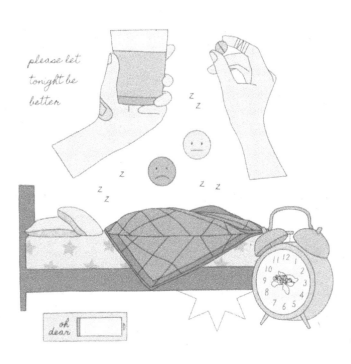

it's not having gotten a good night's sleep in
almost twelve years, despite having tried every
recommendation and remedy going
(yes, even yoga and essential oils)

i dont think i can eat this today

and it's continuous lifelong struggles with food
and eating, and always falling back on the same
list of bland, beige and mostly textureless
safe foods

and finally it's discreet stimming and involuntary masking while out, and melting or shutting down as soon as you get home, all with great detriment to your health and wellbeing

being autistic is often all of these things and
so much more, all while hearing that you don't
'look autistic' from well-meaning but misguided
individuals

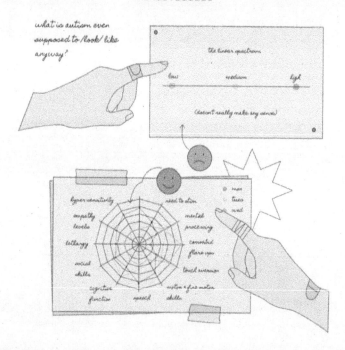

but one of the most important things to remember
is this: the spectrum is not linear!
it's more accurate to compare it to a spiderweb
chart of traits and characteristics that can vary
and fluctuate in severity and frequency, depending
on the individual and the day

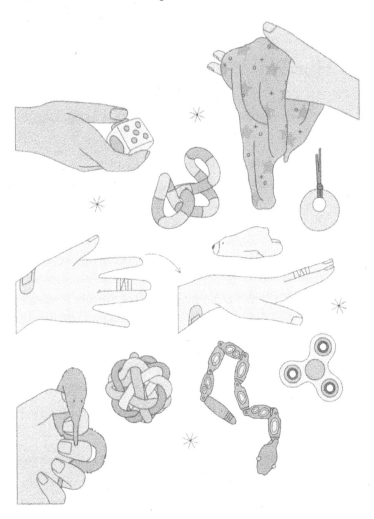

stim !

Hungry

Grace Au

Content note: Death, disordered eating

I hear it first in my dreams. A low, foreboding rumbling like that of a giant yawning endlessly. It's a vacuum for any noise from living creatures. Everything is drowned out by the incessant unnatural roar.

I remember where I am. I remember the floating sensation when we took off, the feeling that the only thing tying me to earth's gravitational pull was this seatbelt with an ice-cold clasp, tightly wrapped around my middle. It feels like a lead weight.

I open my eyes and try to take a deep breath to acclimatise myself to this in-between environment. Plastic panels moulded to look organic and comforting float ahead of me like tectonic plates. Stale, stagnant air fills my mouth and nose. I feel like I'm inhaling the void. The texture and tightness of the seatbelt is bothering me. The roar of the void is bothering me. A tiny fan in the overhead console is blowing freezing-cold air directly into my face when I move an inch forward, keeping me stuck to my seat. I don't want to touch anything. Someone has placed a blanket over me as a kind gesture, but the texture is wrong and plastic-y. I kick it off, avoiding touching it with my hands. I stare at the television screen between the aisles monitoring our position in the sky. Five hours left; I can do this. I just need to sleep. I shut my eyes tightly and try to imagine myself anywhere. Anywhere else. I just need to force myself to sleep through this.

It's so humid the buildings sweat. I pace down a narrow corridor, tiled floor to ceiling, lit with cheap, artificial fluorescent tubes. The moisture in the air makes the tiles gleam. Intermittent thresholds lead into tiny one-room apartments identical to the one I'm destined to arrive at. Each doorway is a portal into a stranger's personal space, open but closed off at the same time. Everyone is sealed within their apartments with a heavy-duty security gate, but with the door open in hopes of catching an afternoon breeze. No luck so far. I look through the diamond-shaped gaps between the bars without being able to help myself, catching glimpses of towels, beds, TV sets, fans. It makes me think of university dorms.

The sharp screech of metal on metal makes my teeth itch. We're here.

Through the openings in the gate I can see him. He is lying on a sofa bed which takes up half the apartment.

The thick padded quilt covers the lower half of him, creating two stick-shaped bumps where his legs should be. Two white blooms crater the surface of his roving eyes. He looks nothing like the gung gung I once knew. He's thin. Too thin. He slowly greets the ceiling in Cantonese as we enter the room. He says my name, so I go to hold his hand. He is too weak to sit up or move his head, but he knows I'm here.

He's wearing a set of old-fashioned blue pyjamas, the fancy type that buttons up and has a little embroidered pocket on the breast. I recognise the flowery pattern from the quilt, the pattern I slept on as a child in this same room.

The flat is miniscule, barely enough to fit two people without causing a fight, let alone three. The kitchen is a tiny utility room with a hob and sink. My grandparents' bed is hidden by a makeshift wall constructed from a huge floor-to-ceiling wardrobe, which was shabbily wallpapered over decades ago. Giant black, orange and white speckled koi fish guard the outdoor bathroom from their undersized tank on the balcony.

Cans of protein shake are stacked up in one corner, like a bodybuilder lives here. I stand on the balcony, the moisture in the air clinging to my skin. There's a lot happening, a lot to process. My aunts are indoors, muttering to each other about my grandfather's infamous stubbornness, the same stubbornness that is currently killing him. 'The man has the will of an ass,' my aunt says, in a tone both loud enough for me to hear from out here and soft enough for it to pass over him unheard. It's a well-honed skill from years of having to cope with him.

My pau pau has kept the flat's shrine alive with offerings of fruit and rice dishes. The red glow of the shrine illuminates the concrete space, a tiny age-old rebellion in the green-blue artificially lit city.

My grandparents believe in paying respects to our ancestors by making sure the shrine is lit and laden with offerings, but I never really saw the point. There's life and death, and not much else. As a kid, I avidly read up on Chinese myths and legends, but as time passed, my belief in these stories withered away. Reality – growing up as a kid of the Chinese diaspora in the UK – became more pressing than fantasy. I buried that imaginative side deep inside myself.

I peer in at the fish peacefully floating in their tank, wondering if they remember me.

I'm spending the night at the flat. Pau pau lies next to me, facing the wall, snoring gently as her form moves slightly up and down with each breath. I'm searching for signs of familiarity online, the phone light a beacon in the shadows.

The air is like soup. I lie on my back, turning my attention from my friends' messages from eight hours ago to the open wardrobe door high above me, used as a makeshift screen for the hallway light. There is a perpetual rumbling of life in the background, a reminder that I'm surrounded by people on all sides, all living, travelling, drinking, sleeping, eating, dreaming.

As I look up at my phone held directly above me, something sharp falls into my eye. What the hell? I bolt upright in pain as some barbed speck carves my flesh, blinking rapidly. Rising out of bed shakily, I hold one hand out in front of me to feel along the textured walls. The same table we had dinner at together seems to vibrate itself in and out of existence; its low-poly shape resembling a video game's textures not quite forming properly. I open the door to the balcony, tears streaming out of my eye, down my face and plopping onto the dusty floor. The fish are awake, circling their tank in an agitated manner. I get into the sweaty bathroom and hold my eye open to peer into the mirror above the tiny sink. As I search, a dark fragment emerges in another trickle of tears. A splinter of mahogany from the wardrobe. I swear under my breath.

Sighing, I tiptoe out of the bathroom, turn out the light and freeze. I'm not alone.

There's someone with their back to me in front of the shrine, the little red bulb softly glowing around their outline. I squint to see the vague colours of blue-and-white stripes.

It must be him. I quietly pad forward, going to grasp his shoulder to take him back to bed, but I stop just before my fingertips graze the cotton pyjamas. My foot touches something squishy and wet, something that shouldn't be there.

It's a piece of half-eaten orange peel with the flesh almost sucked dry. Grains of rice lay adrift on the dark tiles surrounding the figure.

It doesn't sound like him. He doesn't breathe like that. He wouldn't eat from the shrine in the middle of the night. He wouldn't slurp up old food like his life depends on it. He doesn't have the strength. But if it's not him, who is it? I start to silently back away before my foot squelches on the same discarded fruit, and the figure whips round, the crockery it was lapping from clattering onto the wood of the shrine.

Most of its blue-tinged, pale face is shielded with long black hair, but the mouth is clear. The mouth is shrunk to the size of a straw; it whistles gently as the creature wheezes. It's wearing the same pyjamas as my grandfather, and it has a similar stick-thin frame. The entity looks strangely familiar. We stare at each other. I can't move.

It cries. Its desperate wailing sounds like a human voice recorded on a cassette tape, if the tape was chewing itself up. I feel like I'm in a dream, the kind where you tell yourself to wake up and start hurling yourself against dream objects. I would tell myself I was sleeping if I wasn't standing in cold, sticky, disembowelled fruit.

I should be running. I should be screaming bloody murder, or whatever normal reaction it is that people perform in these situations. But I don't. I stand perfectly still.

The ghost sizes me up, moving its head slightly up and down. After several beats, it turns back to its business of cramming leftovers from dinner into its keyhole mouth. I silently thank my grandmother for her habitual food offerings.

I've read about this being before. Is it, are they ... even aware of being not alive any more? A frenzy of hands shovel a peach into its face, those expensive ones that you buy on special occasions, imported from Japan. My aunt had brought some round earlier that night.

I feel sick; this spectacle resembles my own nights of sneaking into the kitchen in the dark, the fridge-door light glowing as I prised open the sealed door silently with years of practice.

My grandfather's cuckoo clock suddenly yells itself into life, breaking the spell. By the time I've snapped round in shock, the ghost has melted away. I stand there in stunned silence, staring at the shrine in shaken disbelief.

I do what I suppose is normal and scoop the discarded rice, orange peel, peach stones and boiled sweet wrappers off the floor. I note that most of the food ended up discarded on the ground rather than in the tiny mouth of the ghost. I take out some fresh fruit from the fridge to put on the shrine, in case it returns tonight. After quietly mopping up the mess, I make my way to bed, where my pau pau hasn't even stirred, and stare at the ceiling until I pass out.

In the morning he's gone.

The following days are a haze of familiar and unfamiliar faces, black clothes and hot tears as the grief begins to sink in. The night before the wake, the entire family comes together at the flat for the overnight vigil, all of us trying to share the tiny space while maintaining a reasonable distance from the body. The body that used to be gung gung but now looks nothing like him. None of us sleep.

It's unbearably muggy the next day. The invasive rumble of the drums at the ceremony is suffocating. I am drowning in grief and sweat until we get to the columbarium outside the city.

The sound of insects chirping out here is an alien but welcome relief from the constant churn of the city. Everything is plants, timber and concrete, 'for good feng shui' my aunt informs me. 'You're interested in architecture, aren't you?'

Each level is open to outside, divided by polished marble walls, which are filled with niches for urns. Some are empty and waiting whereas others are occupied, labelled with the person's picture and details. My aunt whispers to me that they had to enter a lottery to get a space at this burial site.

We gather to burn joss paper currency, papier-mâché food, a paper house. Anything that the dead could need or use in the afterlife, we burn a paper effigy of it. I watch as my uncle throws a match onto a meticulously crafted paper Tesla.

That night, I get up when pau pau is fast asleep. I can't get the mental image of that miniscule mouth out of my mind. I can't stop seeing its bony frame, how its body made the pyjamas look worryingly oversized. After sitting at the kitchen table for a while with a cup of tea, my eyes fall upon the untouched pile of cans of protein shake. When I struggled with eating, I lived off liquid food as a coping mechanism. It gives me an idea.

As routine, pau pau has filled the shrine with ruby-red char siu, juicy cuts of pale melon, and cooked rice that shimmers like pearls in the moonlight. I add a battered can of protein shake and a straw.

Stripping While Autistic

Reese Piper

Content note: Discussions of sex

I led a middle-aged man by the hand through a crowded club into a curtained room, sitting him down on an upholstered couch. He slumped down, his five o'clock shadow shining in the neon light. I closed the red curtain behind us, stepped out of my platform heels and picked up our drinks. 'Cheers,' I said as I handed him his drink. I forced a smile across my face to try to appear flirty and relaxed. 'Cheers,' he said, clinking our glasses of champagne. He placed his drink on the table next to us and fumbled with the collar on his polo shirt.

Behind my wide grin, I was racked with nerves. A few minutes before, I had sold him my first hour-long private room. It was my second week working as a stripper, and until then I had only managed to sell fifteen-minute dances – the minimum amount of time in that club. The hour was an accomplishment – it meant more money and that I was getting better at my job. But I was clueless about how to entertain someone for a whole sixty minutes.

I wrapped my stockinged legs around his waist and leaned my face against his neck, silently counting the muffled rap songs to keep track of time. I grinded on his lap for a few beats, pulled down my pink camisole, and pushed my small boobs into his face, running through my usual lap-dance routine. But the songs passed slowly and I started to panic. I stood up and completely undressed and then ran through the same routine again. He looked bored and annoyed.

'So, where in America are you from?' he asked in his Australian twang.

'N-New Jersey,' I answered honestly.

He nodded and didn't follow up. I realised at that moment that he wasn't interested in my body or my dance routine. When I was encouraging him to get a room, I presented myself as chatty and captivating with my eager smile and flirtatious introduction. He wanted what I sold him on: intimacy. But I didn't know how to exchange pleasantries or casually flirt.

I sat down next to him and draped my leg across his lap. 'So – what's your favorite sex position?' I asked, because I thought that's what he wanted to hear. He fumbled with his collar again and reached for his drink. 'I don't know – missionary, I guess.' He shrugged. I gulped down the rest of my champagne.

'You're new at this, right?' he asked matter-of-factly.

'Yes,' I answered, my shoulders slumping.

'I just want you to talk normal to me.'

I reached for my drink and looked desperately at the empty glass. I attempted to converse, but my chat was stiff, my comments leading into dead-end streets. After twenty minutes, he took a deep breath and got up to leave. On his way out, he looked back at me and I turned away from his doughy face, dreading his words. He dug into his wallet and handed me a twenty-dollar tip.

'Next time try to be more like yourself.'

After I dressed back into my lingerie and outlined my wolf eyes in the cracked mirror, I walked over to the bar and ordered a drink – this time a whiskey on the rocks. I watched dancers around me flirting with customers with ease, selling rooms effortlessly. Maybe I'm not cut out for this? I didn't know how to talk 'normal' or how to be myself in that space. I didn't even know how to do that in my everyday life.

Before I started dancing, I worked at a call centre in a corporate office just around the corner from the strip club in downtown Melbourne. I was hired with a team of eight people just before I turned twenty-four. Our managers encouraged us to socialise with each other – work out in the company gym, eat lunch, and go out for drinks after work together. The company wanted a 'community' feel to the office, which was nice, in theory, since I believed that I was extroverted at the time, but I quickly discovered that social norms in the office were a lot harder to absorb than I thought.

A few days after training, I switched off my headset and walked through a maze of desks and clattering voices to a quiet kitchen. I grabbed my packed lunch from the fridge and walked to the elevator, excited for fresh air and alone time, but as I pressed the elevator button, I remembered that I should try to socialise with someone on my team – better to seem like a team player, I thought. I looked around and spotted Jess, a soft-spoken woman I spoke to briefly our first day. She waited patiently with a mug in her hand for the kettle to boil. I paced in the foyer for a moment and tried unsuccessfully to smooth out my wrinkled turtleneck. I bit into my cuticle, ripping it across my index finger. After a moment, I plastered a smile on my face and approached her.

'How was your weekend?' I asked in an amplified pitch that was too loud for the kitchen.

'Um, it was OK. Why are you shouting?' she asked.

Embarrassed, I looked away and made an excuse about having poor hearing. She nodded, poured water into her mug, and asked if I wanted to eat with her. We walked to a nearby picnic-style table near the office windows and I sat down across from her. I carefully bit into my sandwich and reminded myself to modulate my pitch.

'How was your weekend?' she asked.

I told her about how drunk I got on Melbourne's main drag, Chapel Street, how I lost my friends and ended up at a techno club alone, even how I came home smelly and braless. In the excitement of my story, a piece of avocado from my sandwich missed my mouth and slapped the table. She looked around to see if anyone was listening and let out a small chuckle. 'Oh dear,' she replied. My breath shortened. *Keep to work-friendly topics! Watch your eating!* 'Well, was it fun in the end?' she asked politely.

I nodded yes and looked over her shoulder to avoid her eyes. Jess looked in the direction of my gaze and confusion flashed across her face. When we met during our training, I had successfully attuned my pitch, made eye contact and returned her friendly smiles. She asked for my contact details and suggested we grab a drink after work sometime. I was thrilled that she saw me as someone she could bond with, someone who passed as normal. She nibbled at her pasta salad and peered at me expectantly. I knew I was supposed to continue the conversation but I didn't know how. I thought about telling her about my parents, who were coming to visit, because I'd overheard her talking about her aunt coming to town, but speaking felt like an array of trick questions – anything could end in humiliation. I wrapped my knotted hair in a circle around my finger. She checked the time on her phone, wrapped up her lunch and mumbled goodbye. I counted to thirty before I got up, trying to thwart the shame swelling inside me, like a balloon deflating after popping.

Since I started speaking, I've struggled with the mechanics of conversation: what to say, when to say it and how to say it. I once threw a meltdown before a funeral because I was terrified of what I would say to my grieving relatives. I was only seven years old but I knew by then that I didn't always say appropriate things – too serious at parties or too casual at funerals. I also knew by then what the consequences of such transgressions were: strange looks, rejection, isolation.

To protect myself, I toiled over my choice of words and my level of pitch. I examined how other women interacted with each other, topics they discussed. I monitored, took notes and tried to mirror. I smiled during conversations and pretended to be interested in what people were up to. I repeated phrases I heard. Altogether, these added up to a mask I wore to present myself as someone socially capable. The mask worked to a point – it helped me exchange 'hello' and 'nice to meet you' with strangers, helped me get hired at jobs, helped me get invited to after-work drinks, but I didn't know the natural ebb and flow of banter, how surface conversations build into meaningful connections. So while I disguised myself temporarily, I was only covered for so long.

Later on at the pub with my team, I approached Jess and asked her how the rest of her day went. She acknowledged me warily, her shoulders turned away from me while I spoke. I sipped on a Carlton draught and then asked how she felt about our manager. She smiled and then faced me. I was happy she was giving me another chance after how poorly I communicated at lunch, so I made sure to return her smile, nod and look her in the eye as she carefully voiced her displeasure. I racked my brain for a response but my mind was blank.

I looked over her shoulder at the waning sun and my peripheral vision blurred, sweat dripped down my back, my hands shook.

'Are you OK?' Jess asked. Concern lined her forehead. 'You're very pale.'

'Y-yes I'm fine. I just need to go to the bathroom.'

I rushed through the bar and slumped on the toilet, holding my head in my hands. I took deep breaths until my full vision returned and the sweat cooled. I splashed cold water on my face and looked at my reflection. Puffy eyes. Crow's feet. Gloom.

'I need to get a new job,' I said to myself.

At the bar of the strip club, I sipped my vodka soda and chewed on the end of the straw, careful to keep my freshly manicured hands out of my mouth. My new colleague, Claire, saw my crestfallen gaze and sat down next to me, carrying the mixture of her Victoria's Secret perfume and sweat. Behind us, a heavily tattooed dancer circled a pole around a throng of customers. 'I saw you got an hour. Good job!' she said, taking my drink out of my hand and finishing it in one sip.

'When a customer asks you to talk normal, what does that mean?'

She laughed, spun her chair around and scanned the floor of the club for customers like a pigeon eyeing a beach.

'Ask them lots of personal questions. Nod and make eye contact and acknowledge what they said. And then relate it back to your life.'

I looked at her strangely, my heart stammering in my chest. *Is that how people have conversations?*

'Cheer up, Piper. Here, let me get you a shot.'

She motioned to the bartender.

'Are you honest about your life?' I asked.

'Never. Your persona is your armour. This way, when losers reject you it doesn't hurt. Soon your persona will become a part of you, so when guys ask you to talk normal, you *will* talk normal.'

My head was spinning. I had so many questions but the bartender came back with our two shots. Claire quickly swished hers back. 'But how do you build a—'

She spotted her regular near the edge of the bar and scurried over to him. Last time we worked together, he stayed in the room for three hours with her. What they spoke about for that long, I wasn't sure, but as I watched him hang on her words, how he laughed when she spoke, I became increasingly agitated with the mixture of envy and awe. She flipped her chestnut hair back and led him into the curtained area. I shot back the tequila and surveyed the floor.

The next morning after my night shift at the club, I scrolled through the internet for advice on how to have a conversation. There were mountains of articles and I dug into them fervently, reading tips on wikiHow, *Psychology Today* and *Forbes*. I took notes on how to perfect timing, how to find a common ground, how to show interest, and how to take a light conversation into more meaningful territory. Just like Claire had said, I discerned a basic formula: ask questions, acknowledge what the person said and then relate it back to you. As my notebook filled up with suggestions, my chest began to feel heavy and I grew more and more uncomfortable.

As perplexing and uncomfortable as my social slips must have felt to my customer and Jess, there was no one more confused than me. I didn't know I was autistic then and thus I didn't know there was a reason for my communication struggles. In the absence of an explanation, I blamed myself. Growing up, whenever I failed socially I thought I was just stupid, or even a bitch. I pushed myself so hard to be someone who was engaged and endearing that I thought I was two separate people: the gregarious and genial person I aspired to be and the awkward, incapable, terrible person who haunted me. I read article after article, furious at myself for not knowing how to have a conversation. And yet amid my self-loathing something deeper began to flutter: hope. *I will finally learn how to be the person I want to be.*

'Can I touch you?'

'Yes,' I whispered.

A young man, no older than twenty-one, reached behind me and grabbed my bum. He groaned. I leaned forward and grinded on his lap for a second. He started panting. I slowed down until his breathing relaxed and then stood up and grabbed our drinks.

I sat down next to him and peered longingly into his eyes. 'So where are you thinking of travelling to?'

He told me at the bar that he wanted to travel abroad. I was working through my conversation tactics and thought travel would be a good place to start. His flushed face lit up in excitement as he spilled off a list of countries. I reminded myself to comment on the last country he mentioned. I nodded and smiled into his eyes while he spoke. 'Oh wow, Cambodia,' I said. 'I've always wanted to go there.'

In truth, I had been to Cambodia already, but I was acting through my new persona I'd designed – a gregarious, giddy, wannabe explorer. A few months had passed and that was my tenth private room since the day I combed the internet for social advice. The first few rooms I felt awkward and insecure, but each time I grew more confident. I stood up and straddled him, remembering that I should try to bridge his comment to

deeper realms. 'Is there anything stopping you from travelling?' I asked.

'I guess I am afraid of being alone.'

The tools of engagement were like accessing a key to a lock.
Conversing in the rooms not only wasn't daunting any more,
but it was also starting to feel *easy*.

'What about you? Where in America are you from?'

'West Virginia,' I said without skipping a beat. 'But I love it
here. I never want to leave.'

The waitress came into the room and asked if we wanted to
do another hour. I smiled at him. 'OK, why not?' he said,
nuzzling into me.

The next afternoon, I jumped on a tram and headed to
Chapel Street. I walked into a posh coffee shop and spotted
Jess and sat across from her. I ordered a flat white and asked
her about the concert she saw last night. 'Oh wow! That
sounds amazing! I'd love to see a live show,' I rolled off easily.
Although I couldn't comprehend everything she was saying –
the coffee shop was loud and I couldn't hear all her words – I
knew enough about the cadence of conversation to hide my
difficulties. We conversed back and forth for a few hours,
talking about our everyday lives, then touching upon our
hopes and fears. I felt a friendship budding and my body
buzzed with elation. I was thrilled to display my newfound
social skills. Thrilled to feel connection. Thrilled to feel alive.

It was only when I got home that I faced my tired expression in the mirror. I turned away from my reflection, wrapped myself in blankets and wailed, my exhaustion hitting me like a tropical storm.

I woke up abruptly after a gruelling night of work. The clock read 5.03 p.m. I had been sleeping for twelve hours. I sat up and looked at my puffy eyes. I was supposed to meet Jess an hour later for an early dinner, but I didn't have the energy to socialise.

It had been three years since I started dancing. The first few months at the club turned into a year, a year turned into two, and two years turned into three. I was twenty-seven and wanted nothing more than to hide out in my room and recover from the world.

It was during my second year of dancing that I discovered autism. The realisation that I might be autistic sprung up accidentally when I was trying to get help for an unruly attention-deficit disorder. When I mentioned that I can't switch between tasks, an online support group suggested that I look into how autism is expressed in women. I originally rejected the idea, because while I knew I had social anxiety, I wasn't ready to face just how much I struggled with communication, nor was I ready to acknowledge how much effort it was to appear abled. By that point I was passing as normal, and although I was exhausted, I wasn't ready to give that up. As I came around to the idea that I, indeed, might be on the spectrum, I read a few studies on how autistic women learn to socialise intellectually, not naturally through osmosis like neurotypicals do. I also read a bunch of guides that warned against masking; socialising may look effortless to outsiders, but it will take its toll. I pored over blogs and columns and I accepted it on the surface, but didn't really take it in. I wasn't ready to face myself.

I told people that I stayed in the industry for fast cash and freedom to pick my own hours. But a part of me also stayed because dancing taught me how to socialise. I gained access to a life I wanted with invites to hang out, meetups at bars, parties to dance at. While I was grateful for my conversation skills, I was drowning in exhaustion. Most days I struggled to leave my room.

When I arrived at dinner, I discovered that Jess had invited two other people. I glared at the unexpected guests. I had worked the night before and the last thing I wanted was to mask through a forced dinner. But Jess looked happy and she was my best friend, I reminded myself. So I sat down, politely introduced myself and attempted to make eye contact. Jess tried to include me in the conversation, and for a few minutes I managed light banter, but I quickly ran out of steam. All I could muster were 'Wows' and 'Uh-huhs' with a smile. I couldn't look anyone in the eye. I excused myself to the bathroom where I locked myself in the toilet. Jess walked in ten minutes later. 'What's wrong?' she asked, concerned. How could I explain to a neurotypical? How could she understand that my energy was limited and performing all night left nothing to mask during the day? Would she get it? No. Her energy was never-ending, boundlessly flowing from day to night, from work to drinks to work. I pulled up my pants and flushed the toilet. 'Nothing, sorry, I'm coming out.'

I went back to the table and ordered a margarita and downed it. I felt the edges of burnout threatening to pull me under. I just needed one last push and then I could escape from the world. I ordered another drink and then another. I stopped experiencing. Stopped caring. Stopped feeling. I laughed when Jess laughed. I forced eye contact. But I experienced everything underwater. Finally, I stumbled home, where I turned off my phone, closed the curtains and slept fitfully for days.

For two weeks I couldn't work. Every time I went in, I had a panic attack when I attempted to talk to customers. I had no chat or eye contact. I had nothing to show or express and no matter how hard I tried, I couldn't fit into the confines of my persona. I begged my manager to let me go home and he waved me off, disappointed. When I got home one evening, I wrapped myself in my weighted blanket and a thought crystallised through the sludge of my brain fog: I couldn't keep pretending any more.

The morning birds were chirping by the time my mind settled down. I looked out of my window and watched the sky lighten. I had never felt more isolated from myself.

A few weeks later, I wrapped up a thirty-minute private room with a silver-haired gentleman. I knew I could try to get him to extend his time, but I didn't want to push myself too hard. I wanted to see Jess after work. I giggled with him and then put on a serious expression and asked him why he was so unhappy in his job.

'You're such a great listener,' he remarked.

I nuzzled into him. It felt great to be back at work and have an outlet for performance, the space to be a cheerful and insightful conversationalist. After the room, I headed to the dressing room, and as I took off my lingerie and put on a flannel shirt and threadbare shorts, I reminded myself to leave the performance at the club. In a rare moment of respite, Claire was reclining on an upholstered chair next to me, her bare feet on the counter, her eyes closed. When she heard me pack up my bag, her eyes fluttered open. 'Leaving already?' she asked.

'I'm meeting a friend.'

'But you haven't worked in weeks.'

I explained how burned out I had been, how I couldn't talk to customers, how afraid I was of regressing again. 'You give too much of yourself,' she remarked. I didn't say anything, just stared at her tired expression. 'I should know. I work too hard,' she added.

I smiled, kissed her cheek goodbye and rushed out the door to meet Jess at a bar. Her friends from dinner that night were there. I nodded at them but didn't converse and ordered a glass of wine. Jess flashed me a smile. The night before I walked to her apartment and told her that I needed to cut down on performing outside of work. 'It's too tiring,' I admitted. 'It doesn't come naturally to me.'

She nodded and took my hand.

I watched her socialise from my peripheral vision. I enjoyed being around them but I knew I needed to hang back. The bartender came back with my glass and for the first time in my life I drank in silence.

Handling the Bones

Ashleigh J. Mills

Content note: Abuse, trauma therapy, sex, BDSM, self-harm

Intimacy has always been complicated for me. I have distinct teenage memories of scrolling through the Yahoo! Answers relationship threads trying to unlock the secrets of the universe by reading about *what boys really like*, and a thousand *how to kiss* articles. Even with this added knowledge – and the realisation that I was actually pretty good at kissing – something about this kind of affection felt off in a way I couldn't pinpoint. After a few years of what I considered to be bad but universal teenage experiences, I realised that there might be something a little more serious at play when kissing, the thing I thought I was great at, instantly triggered a heart-racing kind of panic.

I dealt with this alarm in a classic traumatised teenager way – with alcohol and forcing myself to do the things that the other 'normal' girls did. I thought that if I could imitate them well enough, I would start to feel like they did. Unsurprisingly, it turned out that forcing myself into uncomfortable situations was not the best solution to addressing anxiety. Over the following years, these feelings shapeshifted into a helpless, raging black dog inside of me. I was angry. I was angry without a reason I could identify. Not knowing what to do with the tangle of confusion, rage and sadness meant I looked to myself as the cause of it all. Accordingly, I began to punish myself. I self-harmed in a plethora of ways, not knowing I wasn't deserving of any of it.

This all came to a head in my final year of my undergraduate degree. I was much less angry, I was trying to keep self-harming to a minimum, and I'd stopped dabbling with hard drugs and bad decisions. My focus was my work, trying to stay balanced, and my girlfriend of the time. As our relationship started to break down, I struggled to cope, in ways that I thought might be linked to previous trauma. Because of this, I made the courageous decision to put my name down on a waiting list for therapy. I knew it would be a while before they got to me, and this was somewhat soothing; I wouldn't have to address everything just yet. However, as I waited, the problems in my relationship got worse: I would have anxiety attacks over innocent touches, I was unsure of stating my opinions, I tiptoed around her wildly swinging emotions, and during sex I had begun to question whether I had consented beforehand. It took a while for me to get out of that relationship, but conveniently, my therapy began a few weeks later.

My therapist was a wonderful woman called Lisa who worked for a charity that specialised in providing free therapy to survivors of sexual violence and abuse. In case you have not had the misfortune of attempting to find a therapist trained in the area of sexual trauma, I can tell you that it is a gruelling task. To know how to help a traumatised person without inadvertently re-traumatising them is a big undertaking that requires specialised training. As such, not every therapist or mental health practitioner is suitable to provide this kind of help. Before Lisa, I had thought that all therapists would be trained in handling the kind of traumas that might result in PTSD; I was wrong. If you are going to invite the skeletons out of the closet, you have to make sure you're with someone who knows how to properly handle the bones.

Lisa was my bone handler. After the initial meetings to match me up with the most suitable therapist for my problems, Lisa decided that she herself would probably be the best choice as a therapist for me. As an autistic university student having frequent flashbacks at the time, I remember just feeling a profound relief that I would be staying with the person I had been talking to since first joining the charity's waiting list. I'm not great at guessing people's ages; Lisa seemed to be middle-aged, had straight, shoulder-length blonde hair, blue eyes that often seemed grey, and a neutral but comforting voice. She occasionally hummed and paused to consider what I communicated before replying. She asked me questions when she wasn't certain of my meaning. She provided the processing time I needed before gently leading me into a wider awareness of myself. Lisa was – and probably still is – a considerate but straightforward person. There was never any second-guessing her meaning or wondering whether I should be making eye contact. Instead there was a quiet acceptance that whoever I was at that time and in that space was OK. If I changed, I changed. If I didn't, I didn't.

Our therapy room was the basic therapy set-up: two cushioned grey chairs without armrests but with old squishy pillows; a grey door with an *Engaged* or *Not Engaged* sliding sign; a computer desk that held a computer that never seemed to be turned on; a bookshelf against the wall underneath the sole window. After a handful of initial tell-me-everything-about-your-life-please sessions together, Lisa told me EMDR therapy was probably the best fit for dealing with my history of multifarious abuses. Eye Movement Desensitisation and Reprocessing therapy may sound like a lot of scientific jargon, but the reality of it was pretty straighforward. This method contained two things: a list and a light. The former was an exhaustive list of the most pressing traumas, holding about ten items. The latter was a kind of light I had never seen before. It was a thin, horizontal, foot-long rectangular bar that stood on a tripod that might be more commonly associated with photography. Once switched on, the bar showed a coloured LED light, which travelled from one end to the other. The colour, speed and pattern that the light travelled in was customisable. I picked a calming green bead that steadily moved down the bar before gently bouncing back in the opposite direction.

During our sessions that used EMDR therapy, Lisa asked which thing on the list I would like to focus on. While I recalled the event aloud, I had to follow my little ball of green light. The intention is to engage both sides of the brain – the parts engaged in memory recall at the same time as the parts engaged in emotional processing. This is known as bilateral stimulation. After I'd finished recalling the scenario, I was encouraged to try and let my mind go 'blank' and notice the thoughts and feelings that naturally occurred.

I left the first five or six sessions of EMDR therapy wondering whether it would even work for me. I have never been able to turn my thoughts off or let my mind go blank, and even in those sessions I tended to follow the rabbit hole of: *What does it mean for my mind to be blank? Should I focus on not thinking? To focus on not thinking, I need to be aware of what I am thinking first so I can stop thinking about it, surely? Does the fact that I'm asking these questions mean my mind is not blank?*

During sessions with Lisa, a major recurring theme was fragmentation, the feeling that I was diced up into multiple different people. Feelings of being fragmented wound through the memories I recalled, through discussion about the roles I played in my life, and the identity struggles I was in the midst of. The feeling that I was divided up into different versions of myself accompanied me like a shadow. Since childhood I had felt that there was a me for every situation, but confessing this to Lisa marked the first time I spoke that truth aloud. At the time, I felt spilt into many different people: the functional university student who dissociated every evening away, the mentally ill self-harmer, the family caretaker, the ashamed kinkster, and more recently, the newly autistic. I was a plethora of people and they were all me. But try as I did, I couldn't see a way to pull all these bits of myself together. For a good year, my fragmented self was all I could think about. I desperately wanted to feel whole, but could not comprehend a reality where I could be all those things at once. It seemed to be a holistic fantasy and I was bitterly exhausted.

A single session changed all this. There was a voice inside me warning that if I didn't disclose all these disjointed identities, I would be squandering the opportunity to heal. If I didn't confess everything that fought for space in my head, I would never develop the tools I needed to progress and grow.

The conversation began with me articulating the idea that the abuse I had suffered was somehow my fault. (I now know this to be a classic case of an abuser's tactic – if the victim can somehow internalise that the abuse was their fault, it releases the abuser from the burden of responsibility.) My reasoning? I could recall telling my abuser I thought I was 'kinky'. I felt this had given my abuser the go-ahead to initiate non-consensual sexual practices in any way he wanted, whenever he wanted them. I had carried that perspective with me for approximately eight years, right into the therapy room.

When I was growing up, there were no discussions around consent, be that in relationships, sexual situations or with our own bodies. There were no YouTubers with sexual-health channels, or blogs I could access on kink or BDSM that might have highlighted consent as a core foundation. It never occurred to me that I could share this guilt and have it dissolved. As such, telling Lisa that I was kinky very much felt like a confession of sin, something I had to repent for before forgiveness could even be considered.

So I sat in the grey chair, fidget spinner whirring in my hands, and stared at the square table between us. When I had finally gathered the courage to, I looked up over Lisa's right shoulder – as close to eye contact as I could get – and spoke. I told her how I had always been drawn to kink, how I panic in sexual situations without it, how I liked to know how a sexual interaction is going to go and whether I was doing whatever I was doing correctly. I told her how making out with someone made alarm bells ring in my head because I wasn't sure where it would lead, and if I panicked further, how I could stop it.

Imagine my surprise when, instead of informing me that this was the result of a terrible childhood, telling me I was wrong and/or unnatural or to blame for my own abuse, Lisa hummed a little and said, 'I suppose that could also be your autism.'

I sat stunned, trying to process this offering that wreaked havoc with my internalised assumptions. With a single utterance, my bone handler had sucked all the oxygen from the room. By the time my mind had stopped whirring and I was able to focus again, Lisa was highlighting how the kink practices I had spoken about all orbited around the same thing – keeping safe.

Had my mind been attempting to safeguard me all this time? Could it be that I had subconsciously stumbled upon a way to protect myself from further sexual trauma? The suggestion that my traumatised self, my kinky self and my autistic self were so intimately entwined was staggering. Lisa had given me a starting point from which to reconnect the fragments of my self, and I realised that perhaps I was not as fragmented as I thought. The oppressive guilt I had carried began to ease as understanding bloomed inside me. Of course, as an autistic survivor of sexual violence, I would need emphasis on clear, retractable consent in any sexual interaction.

I believe there are three main elements that made kink appealing to me as an autistic person: the structure, the mutually agreed upon social scripts, and the way healthy kink requires an illumination and deconstruction of social behaviours.

The routine of kink – meeting someone to engage with, getting to know each other, negotiation, the scene, aftercare, debriefing – is a relief. It is freeing to explicitly express boundaries and establish safewords, and exciting to know that you are about to get exactly what you want in the way you want it, a steadily blooming sexual tension. Sure, it is admin, but, to me, it is a sexy sort of admin.

As for scripting, kink has its own language of consent and negotiation. These discussions are crucial to kink, in which partners develop an encoded way to safeguard a scene (for example, through safewords), and are, essentially, a social script. Autistic people use scripting – basically a personal toolkit of prepared responses or conversation initiators – to socially engage with people. For neurodivergent kinksters, this internal scripting process is made conscious and overt. Similarly, I realised I could use these tools outside of kink – checking in with friends about conversations, trigger warnings, or even the way my partners and I use hand signals or British Sign Language to communicate during non-verbal periods all have their roots in this secret, considerate language.

Responding to other people's behaviour is the most complicated part. Most autistic people struggle with understanding the invisible steps of successful social interactions. This leads many of us to study past experiences in an attempt to circumvent the confusion or frustration of an interaction going wrong, just like I did with Yahoo! Answers. Essentially we use pattern recognition to illuminate social rules, which helps us navigate difficult situations. In this way, many autistic people often find themselves deconstructing social behaviours.

For me, this habit started at home. As a child, I was always on the lookout in case I needed to de-escalate high-tension situations. Accordingly, hypervigilance quickly became a character trait, which naturally influenced my handling of new or unsettling social situations. In my head, I would build a kind of model that I could add data to – familiarity between people, societal notions at play, timings of conversations, etc. – which would yield suggested responses. I learned to evaluate from a distance before engaging, often through imitating what I saw.

With kink, this habit of observe-then-act is integral, especially if playing with inter-relational power. For an autistic person like me, agreeing on respective roles and expectations before play is a huge relief. In traditional relationships, these may be discussed over time as people get to know each other. To me, these upfront discussions seem tidier, a more logical way of engaging with others. All scenarios have to follow the RACK rules – this stands for risk-aware consensual kink. These rules, combined with research, self-reflection and active consent, have meant I have been able to re-engage with parts of myself I had once thought I was for ever disconnected from.

A vivid mental echolalia I had during therapy was 'the body remembers'. It had always struck me as something terrible, as though my body could never be fully clean when my mind could so easily fall back into the past. Now I know it means that my experiences are simply something I carry with me.

They have influenced who I am now, but they are not me in my entirety. I believe that each person carries a whole world inside themselves. The previous roles I inhabited, and the reasons for them, are all just aspects of the world inside me. I was once unable to envision a future where I did not feel fragmented; now I can see that that future had already taken root.

I'm not sure whether there will come a time where I feel fully healed from my traumas. Instead, I see healing as a slow process of consistently making active, positive choices for myself. I'm aware that I might struggle again in the future – trauma and mental illness are like that – but I have a foundation to work from now. I have a more stable sense of self, periods of past stability, and a collection of self truths to work with: I can be sexual. I can be tender. I can be intimate. But most importantly, I can be a whole lot of different things all at once and feel content – even happy – with that. With some invaluable help and a hefty dose of self-acceptance, I have begun to learn how to be my own bone handler.

Bluebells

Helen Carmichael

I am interested in knowing the path a river takes from its
source to the sea

I love paths. Once, not so very long ago, I was a cross-country
runner. I spent many hours mapping the trails, back alleys,
cut-throughs and shortcuts across the land near – and a bit
farther – from my house. The running took its toll on my hip,
sadly, so my meanderings have shortened and slowed.

Today I am walking away from town, past the red-brick
Victoriana that leads out from the centre, past the small
paddocks with the tumbledown sheds and piles of scrap and
shaggy ponies yanking up grass in juicy hanks. Passing
between two hedges piled high with nettles and cow parsley I
navigate a heavy cement block that serves to keep the narrow
lane pedestrian only, reserved mainly for teens – vaping,
swearing, joking, flirting, shuffling, snogging and shrieking on
the cycle path up to the secondary school. Over the brow of
the hill, I discern the official sign – stating that it is private
land but there is a footpath – cheekily turned upside-down by
some young wit. I proceed to read the map upside down and

sideways, and head up across the field to the brow of the hill. But – yes my heart skips a beat, I'll admit it – I see a new track. A deep cutting-in, tucked behind a hedge wending around the side of the hill. I cannot resist, and so I accept the quest.

Bluebells with a hyperreal luminescence, each stalk a crisp spike, each leaf in a cluster of green blades, poke the cool air. This is sensory overload – I can see every bluebell and every stalk and every leaf. They are legion. My visual field vibrates and pulses – the flowers themselves are almost an ultraviolet hum. The effect of a field of bluebells from a distance can be soothing, but here in their woodland realm, in close-up, they are shards of intense energy pulsating together to form a chorus with a definitive, clean tone. They have a pastoral edge, but it is modern, more Poulenc than Vaughan Williams. I cannot hear them, but the edges of my brain grasp towards synaesthesia. Colour and form alone don't offer the description my mind needs to comprehend and process this. I am high on Nature.

Trees grow close and reach high. There is not much undergrowth. Tall beeches and taller pines crane in parallel like an architect's sketch. The boughs are at their freshest green after leaf unfurlment, and pools of light fall through this high canopy, scattering onto the bluebells and damp soil below. Around a bend in the path barely wide enough for one human footprint, wild garlic sprouts in a shrill white chord – a suspended seventh about to be resolved. I can imagine their peppery hot spice on my tongue from the faint scent of their crushed leaves.

I am alone in the woods, far from my desk and my computer. This is where I belong; this is where I am myself. It is also where I detach from my 'self' and become only my senses. Sometimes thoughts wander in, but mainly I am the rising ground, the tangled root, the sticky, clinging parasol of cleavers and the rushing wings of a startled wood pigeon. I am quiet and alert and open to inputs. There are no rituals to enter the Dark Forest of the imagination: it just takes solitude and a patch of wild ground. Go outside and look around, listen, touch, smell. You are already on holy ground.

I don't want to talk to anyone, or see anyone. I want to be alone, deliciously alone. My head is already full, a thousand bluebell stems jostling for attention, the luminous crackled green of the lichen on the pine trees pulls me in. Close up there are tiny holes where creatures have burrowed into the trunks, furrowed with the bark texture of crackling diamonds, bursting apart and rugged with the tree's life force rushing beneath. In this moment I hyper-focus on the surface and sense the rising sap, the structure of the whole tree, the roots diving down into deep layers of soil formed from old, old leaves and needles that were once birch and pine. Not just a solitary tree but an interconnected web, creaking and bending in towards one another on windy evenings to share their stories of old moss and fungal decay.

I think of some of the 'agree/disagree' statements that I have read in a quiz supposed to help determine whether a person is autistic: 'When I'm in a plane, I do not think about the aerodynamics; I am interested in knowing the path a river takes from its source to the sea.' Strongly disagree; strongly agree. I have seldom looked upon a river without pondering its source.

Are there people who don't think about airflow over the wing surfaces as they take off? Yes, I have the systematising brain. But this does not make me unfeeling – there is poetry in flight, and in the humble spring becoming a tributary, a meander and an oxbow, and finally a marshy estuary where a sole heron eyes me and takes off, climbing slow and strong to get an aerial view. The landscape unfolds fractally from a single reed to a field, to a watershed. And I unfold with it.

My mobile phone rings, shocking me. It is my husband, concerned that I have been gone for some time. I realise it has been close to two hours. The new path took me on a bluebell pilgrimage that I had not planned. I spiral around the hill deasil. I know this land and yet still take a wrong turn down a promising sidetrack that leads to a private fenced garden. I am the queen of 'promising sidetracks'.

I retrace my path, switch back and am disgorged through a metal gate, dropping abruptly into the human environment of straight lines and 1970s bungalows, angular and concrete.

The Strangers

Katherine Kingsford

The act of observing something changes it

The obstacle was withdrawn and bright sunlight dazzled me. I could hear them behind me. There were four, or maybe more of them. Strange creatures.

My mind would not focus. Fear tasted bitter in my mouth as I tried to move my heavy limbs. Some serpent's venom or terrible disease had struck me. It was as if a weight held me down, like wrestling something impossibly huge. The weight was lifting slowly, but far slower than I needed. I needed to run; that imperative cut through everything else. The creatures must still be nearby. They had done this to me.

I could almost remember: a blur of strange colours and oddly shaped limbs, their words incomprehensible, their movements and way of standing indescribably different from mine. Whatever poison they had used made it difficult to think.

I could see a clear path. My legs were unsteady but I forced them under me and ran. Terrible rumblings sounded behind me and the harsh smell of an unknown smoke burned my nose. I did not look back to see if they chased me, running blindly in a haze of dust and panic, stumbling far slower than my usual easy lope.

Home was not far, but in my unbalanced state the journey took far longer than it should. All the time I ran, the fear followed me.

Siku, my little brother and favourite sibling, came down from the rocks to greet me.

'Jura!' he shouted. Perhaps he had been waiting for me. It was getting late, the shadows long between the stones, and he would have expected me back long ago. Even though I am his big sister, he likes to play the protector. Right then I was glad of it.

He quickened his pace, then stopped short in front of me, his eyes wide. No playful grab at wrestling today. Did I look so terrible?

'Jura, what happened?'

I lowered my eyes. How could I answer him when all I had were vague impressions: that I was lifted by strange beings, that things like the needle of a porcupine were pushed under my skin. All the time in the background there was that strange noise, like the chattering of birds as they communicated. I did not answer Siku, I just leaned close into his strong young shoulder when he offered it. I just wanted to go home. The dust had clotted on my feet and in my mouth, and I felt so tired.

Siku examined my neck, looking closely at what the strangers had left me with. I had felt it there: a Thing, a strange new weight. Neither of us asked, *What is it?* One glance between us said that neither knew. It did not hurt but it should not be there.

There was also a raised bump on my shoulder. I scratched it, an itch more than a pain. Siku gave it a quick glance.

'A bee sting?'

No. It had been something like a bee but different. A quick whistling and a sharp sting of impact, then the strange woozy tiredness, paralysing me. My eyes remained open but unfocused, leaving me with only fuzzy memories.

'They were strangers,' I said at last. 'They were strange.'

'You stink of fear,' said Siku. He gently turned me towards the track. 'Come home. We should tell Papa.'

Siku is young, and a boy, he still worships Papa. He does not see that Mama is the one who runs things. She was the one I wanted now.

We picked our way up into the rocks, towards the centre. Siku called a greeting to our sister Natu, and to various cousins, but I simply trudged, head down. Everybody loved Siku and wanted to greet him. He was on the difficult border between childhood and maturity. Soon he would pass his rite of passage and leave us to find his own way; to join a different tribe, or maybe start one of his own. He is not the strongest but he is quick and clever; he could do it. I console myself when I think of him leaving by thinking of him in Papa's place; a bright young leader, not like my lazy Papa. But the fact remains, soon he will go. I keep his company as much as I can while I have it.

The tribe moved around us. Two of the young boys wrestled, testing their fighting skills, preparing for the day when they must leave the tribe and survive alone. Auntie Ooma watched the little ones, who played sleepily in the dust. She would not let them stray too far.

When Mama saw me, everything stopped. The barest groan of disapproval from her made me the centre of attention. All the Aunties, Natu and my other sisters, all staring and gathering in. Mama walked around me, examining the Thing, that terrible *foreignness* on my neck.

'Where is Papa?' asked Siku.

I was not surprised when Mama replied, 'Papa is resting.'

That's all he ever seemed to do, doze away the afternoon while the women worked. Our great lord and protector was never the one who made me feel safe.

'You can talk to him later.'

Mama's face softened to sympathy. She drew me away from Siku, away from any boys, into the cool shade where the women helped me wash. Their touch and attention was relaxing, reassuring, and I realised how frightened I had been. I come from a proud warrior line but today my courage broke. I felt ashamed of that fear and began to withdraw, but Mama stopped me. She assured me that what I had been through would frighten anyone and her closeness calmed me.

I still felt sick, confused and tired, so I did not go out with the others in the evening. I took Auntie Ooma's place watching the little ones. Most of them slept and the rest did not play up. I lay down and let my two little sisters climb over me, a game they always love. They didn't seem to notice the strangers' Thing, that almost weightless oddness that weighed so heavily on me.

When the women returned, it was time for Papa to start the feast; he always ate first. When he had finished, Mama and the Aunties took their share, then I was invited to feast before Siku and the younger ones. Mothers returned to the little ones I had been minding, who then had their feast sucking milk.

When the eating was done, it was time to talk; that was how it had always been. Licking our lips and with full bellies, we gathered.

Even though I was fully grown, I still saw Papa as huge. He always took the highest seat on the smooth rock above the centre, while the rest of us sat on the ground. His hair grew so thickly, it framed his face in a circle. In the starlight he looked at me down his broad, flat nose, but the look was not unkind.

'What has happened, my child?'

I was sitting low down, right in front of him. I knew I had to answer, but I still found it hard to frame the words.

Siku's impatience betrayed him.

'Jura was captured by aliens!'

Papa glared at Siku, and uttered a sound, half laugh, half growl. He turned back to me, waiting for me to deny this absurdity. I looked down, submissive, ashamed.

'I think it's true, Papa.' I took a deep breath, unsteady under his gaze. 'They stung me with a venom that rendered me helpless. They lifted me and poked me and prodded and probed. They let me go but they left *this* on my neck!'

I tore savagely at the foreign Thing, but Mama calmed me. Everyone looked back to Papa, waiting.

He closed his eyes with a sigh of deep contemplation. We all waited, and waited, until we slowly realised that he had fallen asleep. We all snuck quietly away. If he was cold or uncomfortable, he would come down from his rock, but I knew from experience that was unlikely.

That night, I slept beside Mama as if I was still a child. She was warm beside me, and somehow big, even though I am the same height as her now. She is pregnant again but it never seems to slow her down. Always before, the thought of our family, our tribe, increasing filled me with joy. That night it made me afraid. What if the aliens came for our little ones? We would fight to protect them, but what would we be fighting?

The next day, we all went down to the river, a huge family outing. The chance to relax and play with my sisters and cousins was something I usually enjoyed. We always had fun together, and you can get good food down there, although no one was very hungry after last night's feast. There are always plenty of interesting creatures by the river, but they clear away when we come near.

A few of the youngsters ranged away, testing their courage against snakes and scorpions, even though the Aunties always tell them not to. Some hunted small game, honing their survival skills. Siku would need those skills soon, as would many of my cousins when their time came to leave the tribe as grown men. I preferred to relax near the water, lounging next to Natu, who was kind enough not to mention the Thing on my neck. She sprawled out, stretching the full length of her body in the dappled shade of a tree.

We never knew how long we would stay; to me it never seemed long enough, but when the grown-ups rose and stretched and said what a good nap they'd had, and started moving for home, that's when the rest of us started to leave, too. The grown-ups. I was one of them now; I must remember that.

Next season I would have children and become a Mama myself.

That filled me with pride, then a terrible anxiety, as my fears of the night before resurfaced, together with a deeper one, which made me cold even in the sunny heat. What if the aliens had taken that ability from me? I did not know what they had done. I felt all right, but what if their delving had robbed me of something unseen and untestable? The small peace I had found was shattered. All the way home, I watched the little ones chase each other through the dust, which turned to mud when it got damp, and I worried about it.

At home the rocks made long shadows. Papa had already retired by the time I got back. Somehow he could sleep all day but still get Mama pregnant. Perhaps he was saving his energy.

I was too restless to settle, and lagged behind, watching the vultures as they circled, black shadows endlessly waiting for something to die. Had I come close to dying yesterday, when I was in the strangers' power? The thought made me shudder and seek the warmth of Siku's company. I had not seen him since we left the river; since before that, when he ranged away with the other boys. Now they were jostling each other as they settled for the evening, but Siku was not with them. I quickly searched around the rocks, ashamed to worry, but I was right. Siku had not come home.

I headed out of the rocks to an edge where the wide savannah plain was visible. There were a few acacia trees, a few scrub bushes. The vast constructions of termite mounds. No sign of my little brother.

I listened. The world was far from silent, but all the sounds were the calm ones of evening, the night sounds, the ones I grew up with and know so well. It was a few moments before I heard it in the distance, that terrible rumble the aliens made as they left. It was not like the roar of any beast I know, not

147

even like a rockfall. The sound echoed off the rocks so I could not pinpoint the direction it came from. I could not smell the strange smoke.

Siku was not there and that sound was. My gut filled with the slow, sinking terror that he had been taken. That night, as I lay in the warm darkness, I mourned.

Siku came back before dawn. He was staggering with exhaustion, as sick and confused as I had been, but also filled with a dangerous mix of anger and curiosity. While I had fled, my brave little brother had stayed to watch the invaders. He told us their bee sting had struck him in the leg, so he did not feel like running, but I know it for courage. I would have run from them with any wound.

On his neck was an alien Thing like the one I bore. The sight of its terrible strangeness pained me.

He said the aliens were parti-coloured like a bird, the chest different from the legs. They walked a little like birds too, but did not fly. They had a huge beast, bigger than a buffalo, that stood passively by, and they all climbed onto it. Really, he said *into* it, but he must have been confused about that. The big beast made the terrible rumbling growl and the horrible smell as it ran away. It moved faster than Siku could run, even when he was healthy.

Mama, Auntie Ooma, my sister Natu and I sat round to hear his story, with my other sisters close by. Papa, naturally, was sleeping. More sat in the outer circle. As the sun rose the murmurs started.

Were we safe? Should we leave the rocks and venture out across the savannah to a new home, or stay safe and hidden in this one? Who were they? What did they want? Did they mean to kill us? They had not killed us yet.

Mama sent three hunters out to where Siku said he had been captured. They found strange tracks in the dust but that was all. When they came back we woke Papa. It was his voice we needed to hear. He was still our leader.

Now that my encounter was not the only one, now that another also bore the mark of the Thing, we knew the aliens were still there, still watching. Would they take us all? What did it mean?

Siku and I sat shoulder to shoulder, bound even closer by the ordeal. The others were afraid and confused, but only I knew what he had been through.

Papa decided that the tribe would not move. Our territory did not contain anywhere more defensible than the rocks where we had lived and thrived for generations. We would not give up our land or our pride or our heritage. We would be cautious, and move in teams so they could not surprise us.

Late in the afternoon I was out with Siku and Natu, checking the lands to the west, when Auntie Ooma came running towards us. She was older than me, but still swift, even though she had been a mother three times. Her lithe shadow loped beside her and for a moment that was all I saw, her beautiful shadow on the sunburned dust. Then I noticed the pained expression on her face, the tension in her muscles. She was not moving in the easy jog we used to cover miles, this was the all-out sprint of greatest need. She panted out her news and for a moment my world stopped. Mama was taken.

There was not time to consult Papa. I did not want to. I felt a growling wind of rising anger growing in my throat, and it was too big to hold. I stepped forward.

I looked at Siku. He nodded. No words between us; none were needed, the way it had always been. I was always less close to Natu, but in this moment she too understood. She bristled by my side.

I growled from the side of my mouth, 'We get her back.'

No more commands were needed. With my brother Siku on my right and my sister Natu on my left, I advanced. Auntie Ooma was tired from her sprint but fell in behind us as I started off. She still had energy to give. As an elder she should have led us, but protocol did not matter now. I was glad she followed.

The path she had left was clear. Running easily, swift and low to the ground, the distance passed quickly. We all knew what we were looking for; that growling, foul-smelling beast and the aliens that rode it, the aliens who had Mama. As we drew close I slowed and they spread out behind me. I stalked forward boldly.

The afternoon shadows were long. Each blade of bristly grass cast a sharp claw on the ground, a black image of itself. A few scrub bushes and acacia trees were the only cover. We have lived here all our lives; that was all we needed.

The huge beast was dark and had strange edges, corners sharper than shoulders should be. It seemed to hold its head down, passive. Behind it squirmed the alien things. They had some kind of fur or plumage around their chests and thighs, from which their naked limbs and heads protruded. They lifted and set down various inexplicable things. One of them held a square black stone the whole time, pointing it at others as if the creature could see through it.

Mama lay at the back of the beast, on its wide, flat tail. The aliens buzzed around her like huge insects and chattered like insane birds.

I led our group of four closer and closer. They followed me in a diamond formation, even though I had never been a hunt leader before. But these creatures were not prey, and there were not enough of us here to kill them all. So I would threaten them, but not attack unless we had to. I saw no point in killing them. Except, to get Mama back, I would gladly kill them all.

When I was close, yet not close enough for a true strike, I rose above the grasses and the shadows. One on the edge of the group saw me. He met my eyes and froze, jabbering warnings to the others. I hoped that meant they were afraid.

Siku, Natu and Ooma had risen when I did, hunters appearing from the grass. The alien faced us and did not run. He backed away carefully. The others gently lowered Mama down to the ground and moved swiftly to release her. Even in their fear they did not drop her. I respected them for that.

They jumped onto the roaring beast. No, Siku had been right, somehow it opened sideways mouths and they jumped *into* it. It released its fearful roar and horrible smoke and ran away from us.

As they left, I remembered the look the stranger had given me. His eyes were alert and forward-facing, like my own. In them I had seen the fear of prey, but also the respect of a tribesperson. Not so alien after all.

Siku ran a few steps after them but it was just for show. We did not follow. We cheered.

With Auntie Ooma right beside me, I ran to Mama. She was not fully sleeping; her eyes were half open, but she could not move. I remembered that state, the terror of helplessness. Natu and Siku sat watch, guarding us, while Ooma and I sat with Mama. We touched her gently.

Eventually she sighed and blinked, and it was not long before she could stand. She did not bear the strange Thing on her neck. We had saved her from that at least. We went home.

Papa continues to rule, unchallenged for now, and Mama continues to guide him. This season I will bear children and Siku will reach his maturity. And our tribe will endure.

---

www.KaliLions.fic.on

The Kalingehti Lion Project is in desperate need of funding to carry on its groundbreaking research.

The isolated nature of the Kalingehti area means that the indigenous lion population has had little or no contact with humans, making them perfect subjects for behavioural study. As prides in the Serengeti and other wildlife preserves become increasingly used to tourist cars, these Kalingehti lions may be considered among the last truly wild lions on Earth.

The Kalingehti Lion Project seeks to document and follow the lives of these lions as unobtrusively as possible, by fitting them with radio collars. These collars are lightweight and do not hurt the lion. The transmitters in the collar feed back to a central computer, allowing us to track and understand these lions as never before.

An expert marksman shoots the target lion with a tranquilliser dart, allowing the team thirty minutes to weigh and measure the lion, take blood samples and fit the radio collar, after which the lion wakes, none the worse for wear, and can return to its usual activities.

It should be noted that Kalingehti Lions show more than usual levels of intelligence, social communication and loyalty, especially to the matriarch, whom the team have affectionately nicknamed Kali. So far attempts to fit Kali with a collar have failed, but by tracking other members of the pride the team hopes that by early next year all significant pride members will tagged.

Information Superhighway

Tristan Alice Nieto

beep

look, i know it's hard for you, but
you've got to listen to what i say
i don't just say these things because
i like the sound of my own voice
your father and i love you very much
but not everybody will be willing to

Th-Thud Th-thud Th-tud Th-thud Th-thud Th-thud Th-thud Th-

like you're stupid you're a smart

beep

kid but you just don't try hard

Simon. It's Jane, how are you?
Good. no one is going to solve your
Uh-huh. problems for you stop fidgeting see
Yeah. we need to revisit the quarterly projections.
Yep. this is what i'm talking about
Yeah. can you expect to remember anything
Yeah. if you don't pay attention it just
There's no way acquisitions have the budget that
Right. don't understand why you can't sit

I hear

are you even listening to me?

155

More Human Than Human

Agri Ismaïl

For the love of God

When I was sixteen years old I, briefly, found religion.

For years I thought this was merely the way in which my teen rebellion had taken form, seeing as I was the child of Kurdish Marxists, the same way that friends with posh names and banker parents wore Che Guevara T-shirts and had the hammer and sickle in Tipp-Ex on their branded backpacks. Gradually, however, the particular appeal of religion became clear: it wasn't rebellion, it was conformism, and it wasn't God I loved, it was His rules. Having a book tell me how to act in every conceivable situation was (and remains) an incredibly attractive proposition.

By the time I turned eighteen, I had already reverted back to my state of perpetual doubt, realising that sacred texts would not contain answers to many of the questions that I had as a teenager living in France at the end of the 1990s (examples of vital but unanswered questions: How many kisses on the cheek do I need to give in order to greet any given person, seeing as it can vary between one and four with no discernible rule governing the amount of kisses? How do I know whether to call a particular woman *madame* or *mademoiselle* and which mistake will be less insulting? And when, dear God, when do I know if I know someone well enough to switch from *vous* to *tu*?).

I needed a book of etiquette more than I needed the Holy Qur'an, as it turned out.

So when I say that I crave a well-functioning bureaucracy, I don't mean bureaucracy in the Weberian* sense, where state officials with particular expertise are structured in a pyramid; I mean it in the looser anthropological sense. Bureaucracy merely as public organisation.

And, listen, I get it. You hear *bureaucracy* and start thinking of Kafka, Heller's *Catch-22*, Borgesian labyrinths. I've certainly witnessed the absurdities bureaucracy can inflict upon us first-hand: my mother's name was misspelled when Sweden gave her an ID-document and it was such an arduous process to change it that the misspelling is *still her name*, over thirty years later. So when Austrian economist Ludwig von Mises wrote that '[n]obody doubts that bureaucracy is thoroughly bad and that it should not exist in a perfect world', I admit that it barely registers as hyperbolic.[†]

---

* Max Weber (1864–1920) is deemed to be one of the founders of sociology along-side Émile Durkheim and Karl Marx. Weber wrote some books with catchy titles (the seminal *Economy and Society*, in which his essay on bureaucracy appears) and some with distinctly less catchy titles (*Roman Agrarian History and its Significance for Public and Private Law*).

† Ludwig von Mises, *Bureaucracy*, Yale University Press, 1944, p. 1.

In his seminal 1944 screed titled, simply, *Bureaucracy*, von Mises constructs an emotional, one might say hysterical, argument against everything that does not adhere to the glory of the free market, and yet it is hard to avoid the fact that even if we were to grant the premise that there would be no bureaucracy in a perfect world, it very much must exist in the world we actually inhabit. *Homo sapiens* developed language not to chant vaguely racist chants at football games or share their thoughts on the latest season of *Fleabag* but to be able to communicate in order to survive the Ice Age and in time have the ability to abandon a nomadic life for a sedentary one.[*] Proto-religions emerged in all probability to allow for weather prediction and the prevention of natural disasters, while providing an infrastructure for social stratification.[†] As the social psychologist Leon Festinger wrote, it's not an accident that 'from the first evidence of the existence of rulers and ruled, the rulers are regarded as having divine powers'.[‡] The Sumerians developed a writing system capable of representing complex thoughts and ideas not to be able to write poetry, or carve dirty words onto prehistoric structures, but rather to 'keep accurate records of trade goods, craft production, sales

---

[*] Richard L. Schott, 'The origins of bureaucracy: an anthropological perspective', *International Journal of Public Administration*, 23:1, 2000, p. 57.

[†] Schott, p. 61.

[‡] Leon Festinger, *The Human Legacy*, Columbia University Press, 1983, p. 120.

and other transactions.* In short, everything that we deem special about humanity, indeed all that makes us *human*, emerged from our need for bureaucracy.

Archeological artefacts confirm this theory. In the same way that money was developed as a way for debt to be remembered (after all, money's etymological root, the Latin *monere*, means 'to remind'), so our earliest writing consists exclusively of record-keeping. The anthropologist James C. Scott states that the earliest surviving tablets consist of 'lists, lists, and lists – mostly of grain, manpower and taxes. The topics of the surviving tablets in order of frequency are barley (as rations and taxes), war captives, male and female slaves.'† We needed the written word to keep track of a rapidly complexifying world, and the more complex it grows, the more documents and rules and regulations we require.

A brief segue into Iraqi museum history

As I began planning this essay, I decided I would return to a museum I had visited some years ago in the Kurdish city of Slemani, where there is a display case containing little clay rectangles, some no bigger than a child's thumb, upon which there are minuscule cuneiform markings: contracts, ledgers, receipts. A handful of sheep changing owner here, a debt to be

---

* Schott, p. 67.

† James C. Scott, *Against the Grain: A Deep History of the Earliest States*, Yale University Press, 2017, p. 141.

repaid there. Though archaeological finds may never be able to give us clarity on the interior lives of our ancestors, it turns out that they are remarkably adept at illuminating our interpersonal relationships. What has survived of us is not love, as Larkin would have it, but, rather, our receipts.

The fact that these tablets are part of a small Kurdish museum's collection at all, rather than in storage at one of the famed European museums or, worse, looted and sold on the black market, is a consequence of a bureaucratic decision that somehow survived the whims of fickle and often brutal leaders.

Amidst the ruins at the end of the Great War, the victorious Allied powers met with the Grand Vizier of the Ottoman Empire in a porcelain factory in Sèvres to begin the process of partitioning the former empire. The French got Syria and Lebanon, while the British received the mandate for Palestine and Iraq. The Kurds were meant to get a country, but then did not. Documents were signed, photographs were taken, and the representatives left the porcelain factory. Soon thereafter the Iraqi Antiquities Service was founded, under the direction of the British. It was already known that there was a plethora of Mesopotamian antiquities to be found in the region – as the French had been 'exploring' sites for almost a century already (today these works form the heart of the Louvre's Mesopotamian collection) – but under British rule, the excavations became standardised, which entailed that all excavations now had to be thoroughly documented, and that archaeologists could only work on a site if they had the proper permits.

The ancient sites across the new nation state of Iraq yielded troves of priceless artefacts, some of which were housed in the National Museum of Iraq, while others were shipped back to the British Museum, where the British Empire's objects became central to a revisionist history. The cradle of civilisation – as Iraq still insists on calling itself – was folded into the Empire, its objects now part of British history.

With regard to the artefacts that stayed, the ambitious young king of Iraq, Faisal II, ensured that they were spread across the country, in museums that were built in the Kurdish cities of Mosul, Erbil and Slemani, among others. The idea being that the Iraqi kingdom, the borders of which had been drawn at random, could be united by a shared sense of history. And so the objects were decentralised, allowing the local museums to function as nodes around the kernel that was the National Museum in Baghdad.

When the National Museum was looted in 2003, after the Americans neglected to secure the site, the Slemani Museum began the controversial practice of buying stolen artefacts to take them off the market. International organisations advised against this, claiming that it only encouraged further looting. What this all means, however, is that if you want to see some priceless artefacts in Iraq, the Slemani Museum is your best bet.

And yet, in spite of the website assuring visitors that the museum was 'free and open daily 10.00–17.30', I could not see any of the artefacts. As I arrived, the museum stood empty, closed for refurbishing. The lanky guard standing outside the museum with a Kalashnikov rifle hung loosely over his shoulder, said to return in the summer. I thanked the guard and turned back to the car, but my driver whispered a few words in his ear, at which point, rather than escort us away from the museum, the guard opened a series of doors to take us to see the curator of the museum, a kind man who offered me tea.

'There isn't much to see – everything is in storage,' he said. 'But if you want to go in, I'll unlock the museum for you.'

I had, it turned out, used what is known in the Middle East as a *wasta*.

Derived from an Arabic word meaning, loosely, 'a personal connection used to gain something', *wasta* is the fuel of Iraqi bureaucracy, and indeed Iraqi society. A *wasta* is most often used as a shortcut, a way to get something without having to jump through the hoops that a bureaucracy will impose on you, a bit like a Mario Warp Zone, but where in order for you to gain access to said Warp Zone your father needs to have gone to school with a particular Koopa Troopa's cousin.

Iraq's bureaucratic process is almost preposterously ungainly and complex. A few years ago I was in the process of getting my Swedish university degree certified in Iraq, a process which took almost six months due to the fact that the certifying office was only open once a week. The truly mind-boggling part, however, wasn't the opening hours or that they requested a written letter from your high-school teachers confirming you were who you said you were; it was the fact that if the bureaucrat before you felt that you needed to bring more supporting documents – and you *always* needed more supporting documents – they wouldn't just ask you to come back next week, they would actually fine you the equivalent of US$20 for having made an incomplete submission.

It probably does not come as a surprise, then, that in order to get anything done, you need to curry the favour of others. The more clout you or your family members are deemed to have, the easier it is to use a *wasta*. Sometimes a *wasta* simply means a doctor fits you in that same day, but they can be far more elaborate. My first Iraqi passport in 2003 (when Kurds exiled from Iraq were allowed passports after decades of being paperless) was issued without my ever having to visit a government office. I was just asked if I wanted one, and was told to send a scanned photograph to an email address. As convenient as this was, it wasn't an entirely unproblematic process: the signature on that passport is not mine, my name is transliterated as Aekra, my last name is incorrect, and I live in a fictitious city named Stog Holim.

In academia, this form of bureaucracy, which necessitates bribes and favoritism, is sometimes referred to as 'Mediterranean' bureaucracy. This is distinct from the 'Prussian' variant, which aspires to be rigorous above all things, and is the form that is satirised by Kafka et al.[*] The small-scale bribery that is often a core element of Mediterranean bureaucracy is part of a long-standing tradition, where there is a discrepancy between the written rules, which everyone pretends to follow, and the unspoken rules, which the inhabitants of a place are intimately acquainted with, but which confuse and anger visitors. This confusion isn't always benign, either: since occupying forces and colonial empires (usually adherents to the Prussian variety of bureaucracy) tend to lack knowledge of often intricate local customs surrounding bribery, they turn small-scale bribery into systemic corruption, 'serving the bureaucratic purpose of the outsider'.[†]

Needless to say, the arrival of Americans, with their anti-corruption laws and best practice forms, forever changed the region. A society based around favours and small-scale bribes was not great, to be sure, but the dark bureaucracy that has been allowed to fester since the Iraq War has seen the country plummet to the very bottom of Transparency International's annual Corruption Perceptions Index, currently ranking 168 out of 180.

---

[*] Joseph Bensman, 'Mediterranean and Total Bureaucracies: Some Additions to the Weberian Theory of Bureaucracy', *International Journal of Politics, Culture, and Society*, vol. 1, no. 1, 1987, p. 68.

[†] Bensman, p. 70.

The nine most terrifying words in the English language

When attempting to explain to a Kurdish friend how pleasing a well-functioning system can be, I mentioned the Swedish *personbevis*, a population registration certificate issued by the tax authorities. It shows your marital status and your registered address alongside a variety of information that you need to open a bank account, apply for a visa, or adopt a child. In other words, a *personbevis* is an essential document, and I can get one in ten seconds by using a digital ID app on my phone. Even if the king of Sweden wanted to be all corrupt and ask his lackeys to get him this document, they could not get it faster than I can. It is a system honed perfectly into instant democratic efficiency (if we disregard the inconvenient fact that you need to own and be *able* to use a smartphone, and also that the aforementioned ID app requires a Swedish bank account, which not every person living in Sweden is able to get). Instead of being amazed at this bureaucratic wonder, my friend was aghast at the level of information the Swedish state had over its citizens, one keystroke away. As someone who had feared Saddam Hussein's secret police throughout his childhood, my giddiness at being able to conjure up every detail about my life made no sense whatsoever.

His fear, of course, is justified. As the anthropologist David Graeber writes, police are in fact 'bureaucrats with weapons', who do not fight crime as we tend to imagine, but rather 'enforce regulations'.* To accept that armed bureaucrats have access to every piece of information about your life requires a faith in the system that my Kurdish friend understandably did not have. Nor do my non-Swedish friends and family find it comforting to know that you can look up anyone's home address in Sweden. Literally anyone: Robyn, Björn Borg, Zara Larsson ... you name it, they are all a Google search away. And with extreme-right parties on the rise, perhaps I am being incredibly naive in my love for Sweden's transparent bureaucracy. What is convenient today may turn out to be extremely inconvenient a year from now.

It is, of course, easier to trust your government when your country was not invaded by Nazis in the 1940s. Try to implement a national ID number in France, see where that gets you. Even attempting something as simple as a national ID card in the UK was met with endless debate and controversy, until the card was scrapped in the wake of the 2010 election. President Ronald Reagan, honing the long-standing American right-wing aversion to the government during the height of the Cold War, made the bold claim that 'the nine most terrifying words in the English language are: "I'm from the government and I'm here to help."'

Perhaps one reason we instinctually link bureaucratic methods with Big Brother-type totalitarianism is the way that

---

* David Graeber, *The Utopia of Rules: On Technology, Stupidity, and the Secret Joys of Bureaucracy*, Melville House, 2015, p. 73.

the government stores events and, indeed, time itself through its papers and forms. Time is stored through our credit scores, our grades, our CVs. And though it seems deeply unfair to be shackled to the bad deeds of one's past by the time-scoring apparatus of the bureaucratic database, it also allows us to view life as predictable. A bureaucracy tames the chaos of our lives and imposes something resembling order, enabling us to imagine our lives as coherent narratives.[*]

A bureaucracy, then, not only stores time, creating history, but also allows us sufficient predictability to imagine the future.

Roger Federer's serve

One thing that is decidedly not predictable: sports. As such, I've never been much into the concept. I was never what you would call an athletic child, and while I do find football very useful from a social point of view, I don't quite *get* it. Football seems scrappy, sloppy, a pinball game with twenty-two unruly humans acting as flippers, the ball bouncing between them until it maybe, *maybe*, ends up behind the goal line.

The one sport I *do* enjoy, however, is tennis. Tennis, with its rigid lines, its impossible angles and madcap geometry. At any given social event I can drive people a thousand miles to

---

[*] Richard Sennett, *The Culture of the New Capitalism*, Yale University Press, 2006, p. 20.

boredom and back talking about the effects of racquet technology on ball movement, or how the Williams sisters' training regimen changed the entirety of women's tennis, or the genius way Roger Federer can mask where he is planning on serving a tennis ball. (I am not much fun at social events.) The YouTube algorithm currently 'recommends' I watch *Michael Chang vs. Ivan Lendl: 25 Years After French Open Battle*, and *Roger Federer – God Mode Points on Grass*. I like tennis a lot, is what I'm saying.

So when I moved to Dubai in 2010 for work, the annual Dubai Duty-Free Tennis Championship was a highlight of my year. I would often queue up on the day tickets were released and buy as many as I could afford, and sit through evenings of tennis on my own, enthralled by the speed of the game (which is never truly captured on television). On the day of the quarter-finals, after having witnessed Richard Gasquet come back from a set down to beat Gilles Simon, I was waiting for the evening's main draw, Roger Federer versus Sergiy Stakhovsky. The stadium had emptied as spectators went to get snacks and drinks and I took out the book I was reading – Michael Lewis's *The Big Short* – to kill some time.

This book of pop-economy would change my life. Not for its explanation of credit default swaps and collateralised debt obligations, but because it made me realise something about myself. In a scene providing background for the hedge-fund manager Michael Burry, it describes the moment he realised he was on the spectrum, after it was suggested his son had Asperger's and Burry began reading material on Asperger's syndrome. As he goes down the list of symptoms he realises that he is reading about himself: "'How many people can pick up a book and find an instruction manual for their life?" he said. "I hated reading a book telling me who I was. I thought I was different, but this was saying I was the same as other people."'*

As the crowd re-entered the arena and the tennis players tossed a coin to determine who was to serve first, I brought out my phone and googled page after page, doing online tests and reading symptoms until my phone's battery died. Michael Burry's realisation was also my own. The instruction manual for my life was not, as I had already surmised, the Holy Qur'an, but rather the testimony of thousands of people whose inner lives sounded exactly like mine.

Taking humans out of the equation

Dubai would soon have a push towards autism awareness, doing a lot of work to destigmatise the condition, which culminated in their curious naming of the Emirate's new stadium Autism Rocks Arena. In 2011, however, this was still not a place where one got a diagnosis, so I needed to wait until

---

* Michael Lewis, *The Big Short – Inside the Doomsday Machine*, W.W. Norton & Co., 2010, p. 134.

the end of 2015 – when I moved back to Sweden – to begin the process.

The internet informed me that my first step should be to contact my GP to get a referral to a psychiatric clinic. The GP's office informed me that since I was over eighteen, the diagnosis process wasn't really a priority for the health services.

'It can take a really long time,' the nurse told me.

'That's fine.'

'Years, even.'

'I'm OK with that.'

'Just so you know. A really long time.'

I was starting to get the feeling that she didn't want me to begin the process. Eventually, however, she relented and told me to write a letter detailing my difficulties and hand it in at the GP's desk.

'What difficulties?'

'The difficulties you have in life. To see if we should begin the process.'

This letter took months to write as I veered from feeling as though my words were manipulative (beginning the letter with my mother's story of how, as a toddler, I would intone a particular vowel when sleepy, non-stop, until I would fall asleep), as though my entire life was nothing but strife in a neurotypical world, to jolly attempts to show just how well-functioning I was in society (I am a corporate lawyer! I can tie seven different tie-knots!). The fact that I did not know the person who would be reading this letter felt like an extra layer of awkwardness. How intimate could I be? What detail was extraneous? Did they want a fifty-page novella on my pre-teen crushes or a bullet-point list of my awkward interactions with shopkeepers, 2007–2009?

I call the GP's office again, to get more information about this letter when I am told – by another nurse – that I can just write a summary of my symptoms and a bit about my childhood. Nothing about my 'difficulties', which the previous nurse had asked me to focus on. This arbitrary aspect of bureaucracy is perhaps what irks me the most: the knowledge or even merely the suspicion that talking to someone else would lead to a vastly different result. As Max Weber – daddy of bureaucratic theory – wrote, the goal of a bureaucratic system should be the exact opposite of this.*

And yet, the arbitrary has not been eliminated. What's worse, in our quest to optimise our systems, bureaucratic structures are no longer represented by people (who we can argue with) but rather by algorithms and computer programs that decide who gets a mortgage at a bank, who is allowed into a country, who is fired from their job for 'underperforming'. This faith in machines as tellers of objective truth ignores the fact that an algorithm is as biased as its creator – it is just

---

* Max Weber, 'Bureaucracy', in *The Anthropology of the State: A Reader* (ed. Aradhana Sharma and Akhil Gupta), Blackwell, 2006, p. 68.

harder sometimes to distinguish that bias. As infuriating as the interaction with the two nurses was, at least it wasn't an automated message that could not be answered.

For that, I had to wait until I had written my letter and sent it in. The reply came that it was being considered, and that they would get back to me with the next step. What would that step entail? When would it be? There was nobody to talk to any more.

One consequence of having an autism diagnosis in Sweden is that you are eligible for a multitude of support mechanisms in the form of an individualised support plan, including free psychiatric care, personal assistance and access to housing. This makes it less likely for a high-functioning person to receive a diagnosis, as there are government costs to consider. When I am eventually contacted by the psychiatry clinic, I am told that it would be best if a parent could come with me, as they could describe my childhood in a way that I cannot.

Only problem is, my parents live in Iraqi Kurdistan, and flying over for a series of chats with a psychiatrist is not quite on their to-do list. I suggest I talk to the psychiatrist on my own, which they approve, but they still point out that it would be best if I could bring a parent.

And of course I understand the reasons why. Just as I understand why I am not a priority, and why each step in this process takes many, many months. I get why I keep being asked why a diagnosis matters to me (a question that is surprisingly hard to answer other than to point out that it would help me to understand myself better, and it would help others understand me). I get it. There is no part of the system I am trapped in that I can point to and say, OK, if we changed this one thing, life would be easier for a significant number of people. The system may not be efficient, but it is *logical*. I don't want to agree with Marx, who said that 'the universal spirit of bureaucracy is secrecy'. And yet here I am, waiting, unable to know whether my case is moving forward or if it is on ice, whether there is something I should do to make everything go faster. I wonder if the humans have been taken out of the equation or if I'm simply being left on read. I wonder.

I wait.

I keep waiting.

Once More with Feeling

Laura James

Content note: Pet death

'How does it make you feel?' asks the therapist. I get an over-whelming urge to laugh. This always feels like a trick question. One where I have to pull a random word out of the air and attach it to the situation. There is no prize for getting it right, but get it wrong and a dark expression crosses the counsellor's face, like a cloud moving slowly across the sun.

I cannot count the number of times I have been asked this question in a setting just like this one. The high ceiling, eau-de-Nil walls, tasteful neutral carpet. The cornicing, the dark wood desk, two chairs placed facing each other, just a smidgen too close. All are so similar it feels like a scene from a movie.

I have had a lot of therapy over the years as I tried to work out what is wrong with me. I've had the kind where a woman in perfect clothes peers at me over a notebook and says nothing until the silence becomes unbearable. I've filled it with chatter and have been told I use humour to deflect my pain.

I've had the kind where I am asked to imagine each cushion in a neatly set out circle is a family member I am to tell my feelings to. It didn't work, as I kept getting my mother (a green square with a William Morris design) muddled up with my husband (jaunty orange with an Orla Kiely-type pattern). I apologised to the mother cushion for being too exhausted for sex and the husband cushion for failing at school and causing it worry when I came home late.

The therapy here is different, though. My life is different now. It's 2015 and I have just been diagnosed with autism. It is a shock and not a shock. It came gradually and suddenly. It is, above all, a vindication.

I am not mad, bad or sad. There is a reason I see the world differently. Everything begins to make sense and slot into place. Like the scene at the end of *The Sixth Sense*, I see the world clearly now and understand my place in it. I am the way I am because I process information differently. Late diagnosis takes a life and turns it on its head.

I look down at a 'feelings wheel' with a sense of complete incomprehension. I recognise the words, but I am struggling to come up with examples of when I had ever felt resentful, disgusted, loved, proud, responsive, respected. There are seventy-seven emotions listed and I feel utterly bemused. I think I have only ever felt four emotions: the good feeling, the bad feeling, the neutral one and fear.

The good feeling happens when I am absorbed in something outside myself. I get it when I'm writing, reading or baking a cake. It washes over me when I'm in the company of someone I don't need to work hard with. I get it when I look at pink things. The good feeling is pink. It is a pink cashmere cardigan. It is candyfloss. It is blonde hair that has been dyed the softest shade of rose. I love the good pink feeling.

The bad feeling comes in from nowhere, like a sudden storm. It sits heavy on my chest and it is all kinds of wrong. It makes me feel the world is wrong. That I am wrong. That there is so much wrongness that things will never be right again.

Fear is more like fog. It surrounds me and makes it impossible to see a way forward. It paralyses me, like a rabbit seeing a fox across the field. You can't outrun fear. When it has you gripped, you have to sit still until it moves on.

Neutral is my second most favourite feeling. There is nothing bad about it. My husband – who likes life to be big and loud and exciting, full of new sights and tastes and sounds and experiences – calls the neutral place 'living in the grey'. He cannot understand what it is like to be me and not feel excitement. He is older now and his need to chase highs has diminished, but he still has such capacity for joy.

If I had to pick one feeling to live with all the time, it would probably be the neutral one. It is comfortable. It is a warm bath or tea and toast in front of the AGA. It isn't exciting, but it is reassuring and safe.

In the therapist's consulting room again, I am quiet for a moment before blurting out: 'I just presumed they were words writers use to describe a situation rather than an innate reaction.'

My therapist leans forward and looks at me closely but doesn't say anything.

'It is inconceivable to me that people are capable of feeling seventy-seven different kinds of emotion and that they can identify them all and come up with scenarios where they have felt them,' I say.

'Alexithymia,' she says.

'A post-punk band?' I ask. 'Or a long-forgotten B-movie actress?' She laughs, but again remains silent. I fill the emptiness. 'Or a Greek island you're thinking of visiting?'

I leave the session in possession of a new word. I love new words. I collect them. As a child, I would write each new one in a notebook. I would scribble down the meaning and the date it joined my word family. Now I roll them around in my mouth, tasting each letter.

Alexithymia, the dictionary tells me later, is an inability to identify and express or describe one's feelings. It goes on to say that those with alexithymia typically display a lack of imaginative thought, have difficulty distinguishing between emotions and bodily sensations, and engage in logical, externally oriented thought.

Why would one want to think in any other way? How does emotional thinking even work? Where does it lead? If we think with our hearts and not our heads, how can we accurately analyse any situation?

The few years after my diagnosis were mixed. After the initial relief at having found out why I am the way I am, I experienced a slump. Just before I found out I was autistic I was diagnosed with a genetic connective tissue disorder called Ehlers-Danlos Syndrome (EDS). The two together explained my entire life, why my mind behaved differently and why my body didn't work.

Therapy was different this time round. I could feel small changes. I was working with someone who understood me and was able to teach me to understand myself. Slowly I started to recognise and understand a few of the nameless feelings that bubbled up inside me.

I began to experience how emotions can create physical sensations. When people describe being broken-hearted, their hearts really do hurt. When they talk about feeling irritated, it's the scratchy feeling that I sometimes get before a meltdown. Very slowly, it started to make sense. I began to notice that I was feeling something other than just the good and bad feelings and the fear. My emotional range seemed to grow and the landscape opened up.

In working with the feelings wheel I began to realise something pretty profound: I'd spent so much time trying to find the good feeling and trying to avoid the bad that I'd forgotten to remember that the bad feeling (or sadness, as I now call it) is a natural and important element of the human condition. Seeking out pleasure in the pursuit of happiness is akin to expecting your pyjamas to keep you dry in the rain. Pleasure and true happiness are as different as nightwear and raincoats.

Avoiding pain means we miss out on some of the most potentially rewarding experiences in life. It is also impossible. Like trying not to conjure up a picture of a large grey mammal when someone tells you not to think about elephants. We just can't do it. Not for any length of time.

Real, lasting contentment cannot be found in chasing short-term highs, in the same way junk food cannot truly nourish us. There are no effective Band-Aids for the soul. They peel at the edges and fall off when we need them most.

We must experience the whole spectrum of emotion to feel truly alive. We need loneliness to appreciate connection, cold to revel in warmth, vulnerability to relish belonging, and sadness to celebrate even the most fleeting happiness.

For months, though, I had known that a bad feeling had insidiously crept into my life and I was struggling to shift it. My usual strategies of chocolate, coffee, cigarettes and cinema trips failed to lift my mood. Each morning I woke up heavier, less positive and more tired than I should have been after nine hours' sleep.

My children had left home. The last two together. It felt brutal. The severing of the umbilical cord. But surely all parents go through this, and seeing one's children launched successfully into the world must be a joyous time. If not completely suffused with happiness, then at least it should be bittersweet?

Work changed for me. Projects I had been involved with for more than a decade suddenly came to a quick and unexpected end. People I worked with dispersed and the rhythm of life went from gentle, middle of the road, to some kind of hardcore garage funk that felt like a daily assault.

My beloved dachshund died. It was quick and shocking. One minute he was bouncing around chasing tennis balls, his comical walk suffused with joy, and his expanding waistline an outward sign of his enormous appetite for life. The next he was absent. We searched the house and the garden and eventually my husband came in, ashen-faced and wearing an expression you never want to see. Smudge had been hit by a car. Neither of us knew how it was even possible. But it had happened and Tim wore his guilt like an overcoat weighing him down. Still I didn't cry.

I felt as if the world had turned on me. A sharp, burning wound of feeling as if I no longer belonged. I can't explain why I felt it as a rejection, but it was as if fate had turned its back on me.

Sadness springing from the agony of rejection is interesting. It is felt as a physical pain, so much so that it can be lessened by some analgesics. Certain types of types of emotion use the same neural pathways as the pain from an injury or illness. It explains, I guess, why they feel so gut-wrenchingly awful.

My children encountered problems in the real world. Broken hearts, getting punched in a nightclub. One loved his university course but hated living in London. Another found that his chosen subject wasn't for him and he wanted to take an extended period out of education, living on the other side of the world. Nothing ran smoothly. Everything jarred.

The political landscape became bleaker and more confusing with each day that passed and I struggled to emerge from the blanket of sadness that enveloped me. I needed to understand what was happening. Was it mid-life angst? A malaise? An existential crisis? I know it wasn't just me though. A good friend messaged: *EVERYTHING feels so poignant at the moment.*

I didn't cry. I don't really know how. I am envious of those people who can sob messily and let out all their emotions. The sense of loss and grief seemed to stick inside me, growing bigger and less malleable with each day that passed.

Sadness is universal. We all feel it. The sting of rejection, the bittersweet pang of nostalgia, the punch of loss. All are part of the human experience, and to deny them is to deny our very humanity. Without sadness how would we experience happiness? Where is the light without shade?

Something with sharp teeth has bitten my pyjamas. It is probably a mouse or a moth. I think about pyjamas a lot. They are the staple outfit of writers who work at home, but also the uniform of sadness. Maybe it's because it is more difficult to feel sad in a suit. Perhaps because getting dressed when melancholic is way too hard.

I try not to worry about my pyjamas. Even mice or moths need to eat and sadness needs to be felt. Once, many years ago, a therapist told me I hadn't learned to sit with sadness. At the time, I didn't understand what she meant. Now I know that once it takes hold, there's nothing else to do. Sadness makes movement seem too hard, too much of an effort and, after all, where is there to go?

I look out of the window. There is a cat slinking along the farm track. I don't recognise it, but I do feel a sense of knowing its aloneness. I take out a notebook and write down all the things that made me sad yesterday:

- The glimpse of a stranger's shoes.
- Imagining love lost.
- An unreturned message.
- The inertia of January.
- Having to leave the house and go out into the cold.
- A lost book. .
- A half-remembered line of poetry.

- Catching sight of a photograph of my children when they were small and knowing that stage of their life is gone.
- Not being able to imagine the future.
- Watching a politician give non-replies on the television.
- Reading a friend's tweet.

Meanwhile, the world outside goes on. Bits of it filter into my kitchen, through my phone, through my email, delivered through the snow by the postman, and I am afraid to be alone with my sadness.

I've decided to give up fighting my feelings. The battle is unwinnable, so I'm just going to go with it.

I take out the feelings wheel and colour in 'bewildered', 'hopeless', 'vulnerable' and 'despairing'. All contained within the 'sad' triangle. I tell everyone I am sad and think for a long while about writing a book purely about sadness. It is something we never really talk about.

One of the children is off to South East Asia for three months. We take him to the airport and I feel bleak when we get back home. It is the moment I know something has to change. That I have sat with my sadness for long enough. That having four emotional states with two of them negative, one neutral and one positive is not a good balance. I have to learn to feel other things. In the country – alone and in a freezing, rattling old house – is probably not the place to expand my emotional landscape. So, in a rare moment of impetuosity, we move house.

That makes it sounds easy. It isn't. Even tiny changes make me nervous. Somehow, though, I manage to put myself on autopilot and, with my husband, do everything one needs to do to leave a big house in the country and move to a tiny one in the city.

Downsizing is strangely biographical. Together we clear twenty-two rooms and outbuildings. Life's detritus in ten giant skips. We call to each other when we find something steeped with nostalgia. The children's cots, four pairs of tiny red wellington boots, endless photographs, my old school reports (they were uniformly shocking). A pile of local newspapers from when my husband was a cub reporter when I was still at primary school. A book of hideous poetry I had written in my teens. Our youngest child's first skateboard. It goes on and on.

A week or so before we move I wake at 4 a.m. and find my cheeks wet. I have been crying. In my sleep. It is so rare for me to cry that at first I am worried my eyes are bleeding. It seems somehow more likely. I get up to check in a mirror. Then I go into my husband's room, climb into his bed and sob for four hours straight. We are leaving behind one life and going into another.

When the tears stop, I feel somehow lighter. Over the coming few days I notice new feelings creep in. I feel hopeful. Curious about what the future will bring. I look up the words to check the meaning, match the sensation and colour them in on the feelings wheel.

I will always be alexithymic, just as I will always be autistic. And I'm OK with that. I now have so many feelings I can experience and identify. Perhaps more will follow. My narrow emotional repertoire may seem odd from the outside, but it doesn't dent my ability to feel compassion, and there are times when cold logic trumps emotion.

I'm often asked if I regret getting my autism diagnosis. My answer is always emphatically no. Knowing oneself is perhaps the greatest gift any of us can have and wandering out in the world, unsure of why others find life so easy, can be hugely denting to one's self-esteem and sense of self. If I could have one wish around my diagnosis, then, it would be that my autism had been spotted earlier. That I had had more time to learn all the things I have crammed into the last few years, including the important lesson that I am not emotionless. Rather that I just struggle to name and identify what I am feeling. If a puppy were standing in front of someone who didn't know the word for its species, would it be any less a dog?

Thirteen Ways of Looking at [You]

Waverly SM

Content note: Ableism, mental illness, suicidal
ideation

I.

You cry for months. No rhyme, no reason, just one
long-drawn-out scream. You are barely a month old; you
should be too small to contain such sounds. They try everything. They persuade themselves that you're sick. You keep
them up at night, on edge all day, until at last, inexplicably, you
stop. Nobody knows what to make of you. Your mother will
tell you what the doctor prescribed. Her mother will tell her,
when the dust has settled and their ears have stopped ringing:
Maybe [they] just had a headache.

II.

There's an island of old carpet on the summer-sunlit lawn. You
crawl on hands and knees to its furthest peripheries, and you
reach with stubby baby fingers for the dappled green sea.
Nervous systems you can't name sound their alarms all

through a body you don't understand. You shudder. You retreat. The grass stirs as the sky breathes out.

III.

Your mother walks you into school with an apology on her tongue. She tells your teacher as you fit together coloured blocks, silent and intent: *[Waverly] can read.*

IV.

On the worksheets there are circles that are meant to look like faces. A kind man walks you through a maze of conversation: *hello, please, thank you, goodbye.* Nobody knows what to make of you. You try to explain yourself, flapping your arms like your whole body wants to speak. Nobody speaks your language, and they don't care to learn; caring is your responsibility, not theirs. Your father will tell you: *You've got a tongue in your head.* A thousand overawed strangers will tell him: *[They're] such an articulate [child] for [their] age!*

V.

You learn the names of all the different dogs. You learn the names of all the different owls. Your mother records the *Teletubbies* every day and you watch it after school, unwavering in your devotion. You name everyone in your family after characters from *Winnie-the-Pooh*. You name everyone in your family after a different Teletubby. You learn the names of all the different ducks. You love what you love like the earth loves the sun, your whole life in orbit around its brilliant guiding star. You read every book on the bookshelf in your classroom, and you learn the names of all the different bones. You flap your arms back and forth; you are too small to contain such a vastness of love. You run the length of the garden, over and over until your chest splits apart, like enough momentum will carry you into another world.

VI.

You are a faster learner than anyone you know. You learn what danger tastes like. You learn what people want to hear, and what they want to hide in implication. You study the people around you like the smallest anthropologist in the world. There is a secret language that lives in people's bodies, in the air that hangs around them. You take it apart and you piece it back together like a puzzle. Nobody knows what to make of you. *It's all right*, you tell them in their language, and they smile at you, relieved. You learned it early: it isn't their responsibility to understand you. A teacher hands back your homework and declares: *I want Oxford or Cambridge for you, [Waverly], please.* The kind of process that you are functions best with an objective.

VII.

A sleepover, a birthday party, dinner with a friend. You can't drink cola because every bubble is the point of a needle on your tongue. You can't eat mushrooms because their rubbery slippery firmness twists together all the nerves in your teeth. You take too long in the bathroom because it's quiet it's clean it's safe, because nobody is looking. Personhood hurts like high heels. You cry in the dining hall because the constant roar of chatter grinds you into dust, but still you go through the motions, play with your sister when your mother says you should, go outside together when you need to be alone. A writer named Tolkien will tell you how you feel: *Butter spread thinly over too much bread,* too small to sustain the enormity of their need.

VIII.

You think of yourself in the second person. You have to protect what space you can keep.

IX.

You write because speaking has failed you; you try, between sentences and semicolons, to make yourself understood, but you don't show your writing to anyone. Nobody speaks your language. It would crucify you to ask anyone to learn.

X.

You shake apart with relief when you earn your place at Cambridge. The momentum takes you up to school, into the newspaper, into the arms of all your triumphant friends. It does not take you any further. You come home with the envelope clutched in your hand and you tell yourself: *Objective complete.* You are eighteen years old, spread too thinly, stretched too far. What now?

XI.

You cry for months. No rhyme, no reason, just waves of furious despair. You are eighteen years old; you should be big enough to contain these things. You try everything. You persuade yourself that you're homesick. You sleep through the day, grieve through the night, stumble through your classes because you don't know how to stop. Nobody knows what to make of you. Your friends learn to leave you out of their evening plans. You tell yourself, over and over until your chest splits apart: *You are supposed to be better than this.*

XII.

You would be [me], if I could only bear it.

XIII.

The water calls you by your name. It washes away a world of certainties: pronouns, identity, the name you were given when nobody knew anything of you but your scream. You cross the river and you think about drowning. You reach the other side, and you go, and you carry on going.

Resources

What is autism?

Autism is a lifelong neurodevelopmental disability that affects how we communicate, process information and interact with the world around us. Around every one in a hundred people are autistic, so chances are you know someone who is. You may have heard a number of different terms such as autism spectrum disorder, Asperger's syndrome, or classic autism: we consider all these to fall under the wider umbrella term of autism. Many autistic people see autism as a core part of our identity, influencing how we perceive and navigate the world, and the majority of people prefer being referred to as 'autistic' over 'person with autism'.* You may also have heard the phrase 'if you've met one autistic person, you've met one autistic person' – this means our differences and individualities outweigh the diagnostic criteria that links us. There is no cure for autism.

While we share certain common traits, each person has their own strengths and challenges associated with being autistic. This is what we mean when we talk about the 'autistic

---

* L. Kenny et al., 'Which terms should be used to describe autism? Perspectives from the UK autism community', *Autism*, vol. 20(4), 2016.

spectrum' (or Megan Rhiannon's spiderweb on page 98): all autistic people experience life a little differently from each other. In general, autistic people find interaction difficult, whether with the world at large or with individuals around us.

Conversations with non-autistic people can be difficult for us, and the judgement or rejection we sometimes receive when we make mistakes can make it all the more anxiety-inducing. We are often plain speaking and we say what we mean, which can cause us to be accidentally rude or seen as patronising or bossy. This also means we might miss out on subtler elements of communication, especially where social rules are hidden or assumed. Some people have attempted to cope with this through studying conversations and masking behaviour, essentially putting on a non-autistic persona in order to attempt to fit in, although this is energetically very costly and can cause long-term mental health problems.

Autistic people often have issues with sensory perception, either being hypersensitive or under-sensitive to textures, sound, light, smell and taste. Our difficulty with processing senses can even extend into our feelings of thirst, hunger and pain.

Many of us find unexpected changes difficult to cope with, which can mean working, travelling or even leaving the house can be harder for us than non-autistic people. We have also developed ways of coping with these challenges, such as through stimming and indulging in our passionate interests.

Stimming is the nickname for 'stimulatory behaviours', essentially the repetitive behaviours that autistic people do to regulate ourselves, relax or even use to learn about the world. They come in all sorts of forms – hand-flapping, humming, echolalia (repeating phrases over and over), dancing, spinning, interacting with shiny things. These behaviours are often what mark us as 'different', and there are some currently used therapies that focus on forcing children to stop stimming. This masking or repression of stimming as part of wider camouflaging of autistic behaviour can cause severe problems for autistic people, including severe mental health problems and an elevated suicide risk.* Non-autistic people also stim: do you chew your nails, or play with your hair when you get nervous? Perhaps you find listening to nature sounds calming, or the sensations of a hot bath relaxing. Many autistic activists have been working to destigmatise stimming in the wider public, through their videos of favourite stims or stim dancing. This aim of demystifying and destigmatising is core to *Stim*, and why I named the book after stimming.

Autistic people often have passionate interests, sometimes termed special interests, which might be consistent for our whole lives or change every few months. They could be around anything: podcasts, dog breeds, collecting books, sewing,

---

* E. Cage, J. Di Monaco and V. Newell, 'Experiences of Autism Acceptance and Mental Health in Autistic Adults', *Journal of Autism and Developmental Disorders*, vol. 48(2), 2017.

trains, architecture, *Mass Effect*, One Direction – the list goes on. This can lead us to have encyclopaedic knowledge of certain topics, which people sometimes channel into work. In a study that looked at how autistic people feel about their preferred interests, 92 per cent of respondents said engaging in their interests was calming, and key to managing anxiety.[*]

Most people think of a nerdy, scientific, blunt white boy or man when they think of autistic people, partly because the diagnostic criteria was built around them, which meant that anyone outside that specific presentation, especially those of different races, were missed. Black children in America receive diagnoses on average around two years later than white children with comparable presentations,[†] and people of all genders are currently being diagnosed as adults, as the historical assumption that autism was a male condition meant they flew under the radar as children.

How can you support autistic people?

Be compassionate and supportive, and listen to us. Take time to listen to the words we are saying, not how they might sound. Don't make assumptions about what particular ways of

---

[*] K. Koenig and L. Williams, 'Characteriszation and Utilization of Preferred Interests: A Survey of Adults on the Autism Spectrum', *Occupational Therapy in Mental Health*, vol. 33, 2017.

[†] D. S. Mandell et al., 'Race differences in the age at diagnosis among Medicaid-eligible children with autism', *Journal of the American Academy of Child and Adolescent Psychiatry*, vol. 41(12), 2002.

behaving mean. If you know an autistic person well, you could ask them if there is anything you could do that might be helpful, such as avoiding wearing strong perfume when you see them, or giving them space in conversations to process before responding. Remember, we are all individuals deserving of respect and kindness.

Further reading

If you want to read more books by and about autistic people, I recommend the following reading list as a good place to start. If you've been searching for yourself in books the way I have, I hope at least one of the below is the mirror you need. This is by no means an exhaustive list, and you can find a regularly updated extensive list, including a number of great autistic self-help books, on my website: www.lizziehuxleyjones.com

Fiction

Forever Neverland by Susan Adrian
Notes on my Family by Emily Critchley
The Boy Who Steals Houses by C. G. Drews
On the Edge of Gone by Corinne Duyvis
A Girl Like Her by Talia Hibbert
The State of Grace by Rachael Lucas
An Unkindness of Ghosts by Rivers Solomon
Failure to Communicate by Kaia Sønderby

Can You See Me by Rebecca Westcott and Libby Scott
Queens of Geek by Jen Wilde

Collections

Loud Hands: Autistic People Speaking by the Autistic Self Advocacy Network
All the Weight of Our Dreams edited by Lydia X. Z. Brown, E. Ashkenazy and Morénike Giwa Onaiwu

Memoirs

Uncomfortable Labels by Laura Kate Dale
The Reason I Jump by Naoki Higashida
Odd Girl Out by Laura James
The Electricity of Every Living Thing by Katherine May
Fingers in the Sparkle Jar by Chris Packham

Non-fiction

Camouflage by Sarah Bargiela, illustrated by Sophie Standing
In a Different Key by John Donvan and Caren Zucker
Autism: A New Introduction to Psychological Theory and Current Debate by Sue Fletcher-Watson and Francesca Happé
NeuroTribes by Steve Silberman

Editor's Acknowledgements

This book exists thanks to the kindness, generosity and encouragement of a number of wonderful people.

My first thanks go to the amazing Julia Kingsford, who encouraged both me and the idea of this collection from the get-go. If she hadn't planted the seed that not only could I do this but I *should* do it, this book wouldn't have gotten further than a thread of half-baked tweets.

Second thanks go to Philip Connor, who saw my pitch in Unbound's open pitching hour on Twitter and picked us up. Thank you for your enthusiasm and your willingness to go along with my overly complicated financial tiers to ensure equality of access – you just get it, and that means so much.

Naturally, the next people I have to thank are the eighteen contributors to the book. Some of you have been on this journey since those tweets, agreeing to join me in what was little more than a few notes. I am tremendously grateful for the hard work that all of you have put into the book, and I am completely in awe of what you created, what we have created. Thank you for putting your trust in me. Double thanks to Nell,

c. f. and Amelia, who helped look over the introduction and resources when the English language evaded me.

Thank you to all the people who pledged and supported and tweeted and nagged your friends. As I write this, there are almost 800 supporters who pre-ordered *Stim* and thus ensured its publication. You've helped change the face of publishing, and I hope you love this book.

Thank you to everyone at Unbound who has worked on the book or been enthusiastic for it or came over to fuss Nerys whenever we would visit the office. Thank you to DeAndra Lupu and Ella Chappell for your hard work on producing the book; I truly feel that with you it is in the safest of hands.

Thank you to Luke J Bird for the cover – you immediately understood the vision of the project, and I cried when I saw the art for the first time.

Thank you to the whole team at The Good Literary Agency, who have supported me on this journey, especially my magnificent agent Abi Fellows. It is truly wonderful to work with a group of people you so wholeheartedly admire.

Thank you to Queer Tears, Anxious Pep Corner, alt Twitter, Soft Hog Babes and all my other friends both on and offline for putting up with the constant percentage or editing chat for the last two years. Thank you to my parents Aliy and Keith, my sister Julie and brother-in-law James, my in-laws Mary-Ann and Derek, Geoff and Steph, and my niblings Leon, Dylan, Poppy and Theo for your encouragement, love and support.

Editor's Acknowledgements

Thank you to Nerys for putting up with me, especially when you wanted to play and I was deep in editing or reading the book out loud when you wanted to sleep. I'll buy you a big treat to make up for it.

My final thanks go to my wonderful partner Tim, who has supported me through getting my autism diagnosis and a complete career change towards books, as well as putting up with all the stacks of *Stim* in various stages around the house. You changed my world for the better.

The Contributors

Grace Au (them/they) is an architecture student and amateur gardener. They spend their time thinking about cities, mental health, folk horror, anarchism and social housing. Their writing is featured in *On Anxiety* from 3 of Cups Press.

Nell Brown edits other people's words for a living but is getting into writing her own. Over the past ten years she's worked for various organisations, from an art gallery to a health charity, making sure the information they publish online is accessible, accurate and interesting.

Helen Carmichael is a video game designer and has created two titles set in Georgian England, *Shadowhand* and *Regency Solitaire*, as well as a challenging combat card game, *Ancient Enemy*. She works with her husband in their small company, Grey Alien Games, and has done a fair amount of PR dressed as a highwaywoman. She also worked for many years as a science writer and editor. Her interests include sustainable fashion and hedgerow herbalism. She lives in Dorset and has two children.

Mrs Kerima Çevik's activism is informed by the Albert Camus quote 'The purpose of a writer is to keep civilization from destroying itself.' She writes, speaks and leverages social media to effect transformative change in areas of critical race, intersectionality, restorative justice and improving quality of life in services and supports for nonspeaking Black autistics throughout their lives. She is an independent researcher who strives to emphasise disparities in quality of life for marginalised intersected disabled populations and their families because she believes that these disparities can be resolved in her lifetime through grassroots community-building activities, restorative justice, trauma-informed care, and pay-it-forward activism models. She has a background in legislative advocacy and social media advocacy, including her Autism Training Bill and the viral #AutisticWhileBlack hashtag. She is a married multilingual and multiracial mother of two children, currently homeschooling her teenaged son Mustafa, a nonspeaking high support needs autistic teen able to communicate through a combination of AAC sign language and his own gestural language.

Lizzie Huxley-Jones is a writer and editor based in London. She can be found editing at independent micropublisher 3 of Cups Press, and she also advises writers as a freelance sensitivity reader and consultant. In her past career lives, she has been a research diver, a children's bookseller and a digital communications specialist. She tweets too much at @littlehux, taking breaks to walk her dog Nerys.

Agri Ismaïl is a Kurdish author, based in Sweden. His work has appeared in *The White Review*, *Asymptote* and *Guernica*, amongst other places. He was longlisted for the 2017/2018 Galley Beggar Press Short Story Prize, was a runner-up for the 2017 Lifted Brow & RMIT non/fictionLab Prize for Experimental Non-Fiction, and his piece 'Haunted Home' won the 2016 Stack Award for best non-fiction.

Laura James is a journalist, author and columnist whose work has appeared in many national and international newspapers and magazines. She is the author of nine books. The latest, *Odd Girl Out*, is a memoir on being autistic. She campaigns for autism awareness, lives in Norfolk and has four children.

Katherine Kingsford is an actor, playwright and potter who lives in the West Country. She was diagnosed as autistic when she was thirty-two though she was first referred for psychiatric evaluation when she was seven and has spent many years struggling with how she fits into the world, due to her lack of diagnosis. Writing and telling stories have been a constant source of joy in her life. Her book, *Asperger's and Asparagus*, co-written with her sister Julia, about their life growing up with her undiagnosed autism, will be published by Bluebird Books in 2020.

Rachael Lucas is an author of books for adults and teenagers. Her Carnegie Medal-nominated young adult novel *The State of Grace* features an autistic protagonist, and was selected by the IBBY International Committee as an Outstanding Book for Young People with Disabilities. Rachael lives by the seaside in the north-west of England with her family and an ever-growing menagerie of animals. She's currently working on her tenth book. For news and updates, visit www.rachaellucas.com

Ashleigh J. Mills is a queer, agender, Black femme. When executive functioning isn't besting them, they are usually attempting to find ways to blend their academic background with their special interests. This usually manifests as being an outspoken Black activist, researching their special interests (autism, psychology, trauma, sexuality, gender and kink), and writing about them in a more accessible, relatable way. When that isn't possible, their thoughts and experiences are expressed through overly personal tender poetry that focuses on radical softness in the face of adversity. You can find them at AshleighJMills.com or on Twitter and Instagram @ashleighjmills

Tristan Alice Nieto is a writer and filmmaker living in London. Her work explores contemporary notions of identity and how it intersects with technology, cultural conditions and politics. Tristan spent her formative years in Melbourne, Australia, pretending to enjoy parties, the sun and Britpop. When she's not working (which is never) she can usually be found at home, trapped under a sleeping cat whilst reading Wikipedia pages about Victorian-era medical procedures. Tristan's work for *Stim* explores a specific moment of sensory overload from her childhood.

The Contributors

Reese Piper is a stripper, writer and journalist based in New York. She writes about the laws and stigma sex workers face, as well as her experiences living as a messy autistic woman. Like most women, she found out about autism as an adult and it changed her world for the better. Every day she learns something new about how autism has shaped her identity and she tries to incorporate that self-discovery into her writing. Her work has been featured in the *Establishment*, *Upworthy*, *Motherboard*, the *New Orleans Advocate*, *Ravishly* and more.

c. f. prior is a writer, editor & digital producer. They write about art, literature, film, queerness & water. They have written for *Art Quarterly*, *PYLOT*, the *Leopard* and more. They are also a non-fiction editor with 3 of Cups Press, whose first book came out in February 2018.

Megan Rhiannon is an autistic illustrator and Cambridge School of Art graduate, currently based and freelancing in London. Her work is inspired by her day-to-day life and experiences, as well as her varied interests and a deep enthusiasm for learning and adventuring. Alongside her illustrative work, she is an avid photographer, planner enthusiast and compulsive notebook keeper. She is keen on detail and on creating work to document and express. Her work can be seen here: www.megan-rhiannon.com

Robert Shepherd has always found the world confusing, and writes to try and help it make more sense to himself and others. You can find more of his writing here: itsrobertsblog. blogspot.co.uk

Waverly SM is a writer, internet-dweller and ocean person trying to approximate the anchorite lifestyle in Oxford. They're a 2019 Lambda Literary Fellow, and have worked with prominent queer writers including Benjamin Alire Sáenz (*Aristotle and Dante Discover the Secrets of the Universe*). Prior to that, they studied English Literature at the University of Cambridge, where they worked on Tennessee Williams' early plays, on medieval saints' lives, and on not having a breakdown debilitating enough to get them kicked out. Their work can be found at www.waverlysm.com

After an MA in Creative Writing, **Amelia Wells** has written nothing useful for ten years. They spend their time making book-themed candles as Amelia's Kitchen Candles, walking around the Devil's Punchbowl, thinking about tidying the flat, and otherwise carving out a small, comfortable life. They are anxious, autistic, queer, bi and furious. You can buy their candles here: www.etsy.com/uk/shop/AmeliaKitchenCandles

gemma williams is a late-diagnosed autistic thinker, maker, beekeeper and boat-dweller, currently undertaking a Ph.D. in Linguistics, researching autistic language use. She spent several years writing and recording avant-garde folk-pop as 'Woodpecker Wooliams', gaining support from the *Guardian*, the *Sunday Times* and the *Independent*, among others, and performing at Yoko Ono's Meltdown festival (www.gemmawilliamsmusic.co.uk). This short story explores one type of autistic sensual-sexuality and themes of unbelonging.

Tjallien de Witte is a fine artist who loves to draw. Her favourite tools include pen, ink and graphite. Her work is inspired by nature, with fluids and dynamic systems in motion in particular. Besides the artistic side, art is also a tool to deal with everyday life on the autism spectrum and a way to calm down with the repetitive nature of her drawings. She is most active on Instagram with the name @brimstodial, where she shares the process of her artworks.

Unbound is the world's first crowdfunding publisher, established in 2011.

We believe that wonderful things can happen when you clear a path for people who share a passion. That's why we've built a platform that brings together readers and authors to crowdfund books they believe in – and give fresh ideas that don't fit the traditional mould the chance they deserve.

This book is in your hands because readers made it possible. Everyone who pledged their support is listed below. Join them by visiting unbound.com and supporting a book today.

Heather Belmonte
Amber Benbow
Calum Bennett
Rebecca Benson
Rob Benyer
Tim Berry
Anna Bewick
Suzanne Bhargava
Elouise Sylvia
    Bingham
Julian Birch
Birdie
Carolyn Black
Debra Black
Eliza Blair
Ewen Blair
Clare Kathleen Bogen
Alex Bollard
Gavin Bollard
Becky Bolton
Rupi Bond
Amy Borsuk
Amand Bow
Jade Boylan
Ka Bradley
Martha Bradley
Alice Bradnack
Jasmin Brandram Jones
Stephanie Bretherton
Adrian Briggs
Emma Britton
Iain Broadfoot
Chris Broadhurst
Creighton Broadhurst

Isabelle Broqua
Carmella Brown
Louise Brown
Mark Brown
Brian Browne
Lianne Burbage
Stephanie Burgis
Hannah Burgoyne
Kimberly Burke
Kat Burkinshaw
Nicole Burstein
PA C
Zoe C
Elizabeth Cady
Lillian Cairns
D Caius
Jen Campbell
Carlyn Campbell-
    Johannes
Helen Carmichael
Maddi Caro
Melanie Carr
Stacey Carr
Sarah Carter
Joe Catcheside
Emily Catchpole
Robin Catchpole
Ann Chalkley
Mike Challis
Ollie Chamberlain
Dean Chambers
Emma Champion
Valerie Chang
Emma Chapman

Laura Charlton
Nolan Check
Annie ChestKnee
Paul Child
Alex Chisholm
Hannah-Maria
    Chisholm
Rebecca Christie
Declan Clancy
Louise Clancy
Bethan Clark
Oliver Clark
Scarlet Clark
Alex Clarke
Eliza Clarke
LC Clarke
Shannon Clarke
Jo Clayton
Douglass Clem
Audrey Clemenson
Felicity Cloake
Dave Coates
Anna Coatman
Patrick Collier
Tomas Conefrey
Kirsty Connell-Skinner
Suzanne Connor
James Cook
Jude Cook
Laura Cooper
Robert Cooper
Jasmine Cope
Eoin Corbett
Thomas Corker

Katharine and
  Elizabeth Corr
Sarah Corrigan
Camilla Crabtree
Ellie Craven
Kenneth Cross
Aiden Crossman
Sarah Crown
Julia Croyden
Alice Cruickshank
Hannah Cullen
Alexander Cunliffe
Kalan D
Gaudi Daamen
Diana Dagadita
Penny Dakin-Kiley
Philippa Daniels
Brian Davidson
Ben Davies
Steph Davies
Shona Davison
Susie Day
Hanah De Laurell
Sj de Witte
Tjallien de Witte
Michelle Dee
Simon Demissie
Joe Devine
Julie Devon
G. Deyke
Dianaki
Andrew Dodd
James Doddington
Kirsty Doole

Nish Doshi
Georgina Downard
Declan Downey
Lizzy Doxsey
Amanda Drabek
Charlotte Dreyfus
Jacob Drum
Mary Duffy
Natalie Duffy
Sarah Duncan
Laura Ellen Dunford
Katherine Dunn
Katharine Durrant
Imogen Dyer
Miss E.
Brandon Eaker
Kathryn Eastman
Charlie Edmunds
Claire Edwards
Elio
Julia Elliot
Laura Elliott
Mair Elliott
Ashley Elsdon
Julie Emmanuel
Chloe Erin
Theresa Evans
Megan Farr
Finbarr Farragher
Vaya Fatima
Theresa Feetenby
Madeleine Fenner
Emma Ferrier
Alice Field

Rees Finlay
Dermot Fitzsimons
Liz Flanagan
Matthew Flanagan
Jane Flynn
Alexandra Forshaw
Anna Foster
Stephanie Foulds
Chelsea Fowler
Kate Fox
Luke Fox
Ruth Franklin
Emma Fredrick
Esmi Freeman
Jaca Freer
Naomi Frisby
Peter Fullagar
Helen Fuller
Anwen G
Aisling Gallagher
Lindsay Galvin
CL Gamble
Savan Gandecha
Matthew Gardner
Christine Garland
Charlie Garner
Sarah Garnham
Jamie Gay
Claire Genevieve
Brice Gensburger
Shaun Gibbons
Jonathan Gibbs
Daniele Gibney
Sheila Gibson

Stoodley
Harry Josephine Giles
Graham Gilligan
GMarkC
Edward Gold
Lily Golding
Barbara Gonzalez Baz
Lindsey Gordon
Julie Gough
Dian Maisie Otter
    Grace
Katie Graham
TheoJane Graham
Kenneth Gray
Laurie Green-Eames
Lucy Greenwood
Jay Gregory
James Gregory-Monk
Erin Grev
Rhys Grey
Em Griffith
Kirsten Griffith
Hugh Griffiths
Chris Grollman
Lou Guillou
Anisha Gupta
Jasper Xander
    Gwaltney-Pease
Rei Haberberg
Alice Hack
Grace Hagger
Daniel Hahn
Gemma Haley
Ellen Hall

Nathan Halsall
Mary Hamilton
Courtney Hammett
Aidan Hanratty
Ole Kristian
    Hanshaugen
Vibeke Hanshaugen
    Lunder
Jodie Hare
Georgia Harper
Matthew Harper
Becca Harper-Day
Gareth Harris
Jenny Harris
Abby Harrison
Kate Harrison
Peter Harrison
David Hartley
Cassidy Hartwig
Colin Harvey
Raisa Hassan
Freya Hausotte
Maximilian Hawker
Kellyn Hawley
Milla Hawley
Alex Hawthorne
Frances Haynes
Sam Haysom
Anwen Hayward
Coral Heath
Katherine Helme
Jessie Hewitson
Angelina Hewitt
Siân Hewitt

Kat Hewlett
David Heyman
Noah Grace Hoar
Roo Hocking
Susan Hodgkinson
Megan Holland
Kate Holmden
Ailsa Holmes
Emily Howell
Emily Huffman
Catherine Hunt
Siân Hunter
Leisha Hussien
Kim Hutson
Stephanie Hutton
Graham Huws
Icon Books
Jennifer Iden
Henry Indorato
Marcus Inthavong
Miranda Iossifidis
Simona Irish
Diana Jackson
Anna Rose James
Lauren James
Natalie James
Robin Jax
Adam Jeal
Haley Jenkins
Stacey Jenkins
Ed Jennings
Callum Jessamine
Krishanthi Jeyakumar
AJ Joers

Miranda Johansson
Colin Johnson
Emmy Maddy
   Johnston
Rob Johnston
Tzipporah Johnston
Ardal Jones
Frankie Jones
Keith & Aliy Jones
Manda Jones
Nelson Jones
Siân Jones
Vanessa Jones
Mike Jung
T K
Manveer Singh
   Kahlon
Wei Ming Kam
J Kampinga
Kathryn Kaupa
Clouds Kay
Erin Kelly
Juliet Kemp
Emma Kennedy
Laine Kenton
Katie Khan
Mobeena Khan
Dan Kieran
Matt Killeen
Melanie Kimble
Alana King
Matt King
Julia Kingsford
Sam Kischkel

Michael Kitchen
Ed Knock
Rae Knowler
Julia Königs
John Koshy
Rachel Kowert
Sonja Krause-Harder
Dzmitry Kushnarou
Paul La Planche
John-James Laidlow
Kirstin Lamb
Vivianne Langdon
Sara Langston
John Lapsley
Fion J. Lau
Lynne Laverty
Patrice Lawrence
Caroline Lee
Effy Lee
Sarah Lee
Alice Leiper
Hanne-Kristin
   Schrøder Leiros
Georgia Lennie
Victoria Lennon
Ash Li
Jason Li
Chris Limb
Pieter Limberger
Joanne Limburg
Katie Linden
David Lingard
Benedict & Jane
   Lintott

Katherine Litman
Mike Little
Samuel J Little
Polina Litvak
Sarah Lloyd
Eva Llurda Bosch
Kate Lockwood
   Jefford
Caitlin Lomas
Emma Lord
Chris Love
Pax Lowey
Rachael Lucas
Erica Lynne
Anna M
Jaclyn M
Abi Mabbutt
Scott Mabbutt
Alyson Macdonald
Anna Machell
Lydia Mackay
Ellen Mackenzie
Chris Mackie
Stuart Mackie
Nicole Maddock
Lucy Magoolagan
Susan Magoolagan
Hannah Maguire
Emma Maher
Madeline Maher
Sylvie Maher
Sumita Majumdar
Sharon Manship
Paul Marlow

Supporters

Ita Marquess
Jade Mars
Helen Marsh Jeffries
Chris and Nancy
   Marshall
Ophelia Marshall
Steve Marshall
Anna Mason
Carole Mattar
Janina Matthewson
Manar Matusiak
Katherine May
Selina Mayer
Kelly McAnena
Erin McCarthy
Nicky McCarthy
Fraser McCormick
Rebecca McCormick
Christina McDermott
Cat McGill
Abby McGrath
Emer McHugh
Kirsteen McNish
Barbara Joan Meier
Alex Melichar
Narayani Menon
Julie Meredith
Tom Metcalfe
Mike Meynell
Emerson Milford
   Dickson
Fiona Miller
Michelle Mirick
Bryan Mitchell

Cat Mitchell
David Mitchell
Montanna Mitchell
Scott Mitchell
John Mitchinson
Lucy Moffatt
Virginia Moffatt
RicMtheGM&
   TheAzlanti Ric
   Mohri
Jorik Mol
Eleanor Mollett
Alastair Monk
Olivia Montoya
Sean Moore
Sparrow Moore
Glyn Morgan
Guy Morgan
Charlotte Morris
Joanna Morris
Sue Morton
Alys Mumford
Aisling Murphy
Ali Murphy
Oolong Murray
Jamie-Lee Nardone
Carlo Navato
Ether Nepenthes
Anna Nicholson
Maria Niemel
Emily Niner
Laura Noakes
Lorraine Nolan
Sharon Nolan

Jordan Norris
Neil Norris
Badger North
Eleanor Norton
Hervé Nourisson
Jasper Nyman
Sarah O'Brien
Kerry O'Connell
Shona O'Keeffe
Louise O'Mahony
Mairen O'Shea
Laura Oliver
Elodie Olson-Coons
Emily Oram
Bridget Orr
Fiz Osborne
Alice Oseman
Nicola Owen
Sarah Page
Lev Parikian
Aaron Parker
Nicky Parker
Stephanie Parker
Thomas Paschal
Ashita Patel
Kristin Patterson
Emma Pattinson
Paul inaspectrum.com
Emma Payne
pbz1912
Helen Peavitt
Aliisa Percival
Ely Percy
Ella Perry

Vanessa Peterson
Tom Petrosino
Het Phillips
Flore Picard
Dave Pickering
Kath Pierce
Phil Pierce
Neal Pike
Jack Pinnington
Chelsey Pippin
Clemency Pleming
Justin Pollard
Samuel Pollen
Elysia Ponzetta
Andrew Pople
Selina Postgate
Holly Potier
Jackie Potter
Lorne Power
Lucy Power
Amy Powis
Lucy Powrie
Tina Price-Johnson
Megan Priestley
María Prieto Berzal
Laura Prost
Pruney
Melissa Pschigoda
Christina Pullman
Judith Pullman
Alice-May Purkiss
Tom Purser
Philip Purser-Hallard
Ruth Quinlan

Amy Quinn
Pablo R
Jody Rae
Jennifer Rainbow
Eli Rainsberry
Alice Ralph
Marion Rankine
Raptorbricks
Amy Rawe
Natalie Read
Jenny Reid
Louise Reid
Megan Rhiannon
Jonathan Richards
Jo Richardson
Mark Ridgway
Liam Riley
Paul Ringkamp
Jay Rishel
Duncan Ritchie
Adelaide Robinson
Charlotte Robinson
Elle Robinson
Sallyanne Rock
Katie Roden
Charlie Rodgers
Samantha Rogers
Ryan Rognas
Vincent Rökaeus
Riley Rose
Zebra Rose
Rachel Rowan Olive
Aurélie-Gabrielle Ruas
Lydia Ruffles

Jonathan Ruppin
Amy Rush Da Silva
Laurence Russell
Hayley Rutland-
    Walker
Scott Rux
Cos Ryan
Luke Ryan
Saba Salman
Marjory Samdojtez
Rosa Samhain
Luke Sargent
Lucy Saxon
Pascale Scheurer
Jenny Schwarz
Heather Sciacca
Karen Scorer
Will Scotland
Fiona Scott
Tom Scott
Olivia Scott-Berry
Nina Seale
Laura Seymour
Tia Shafee
Samantha Shannon
Jesse Sharad
Greg Shaw
Hazel Nico Shaw
Richard Sheehan
Isobel Sheene
Ron Sherrington
Shelley Shocolinsky-
    Dwyer
Anna Sikorska

Supporters

Ceillie Simkiss
John Simmonds
Graeme Simsion
James Sinclair
Kier Sinclair
David Singh
Kathryn Slater
Catherine Smillie
Lindsey Sminks
Georgina Smith
Lou Smith
Tristan Smith
Ben Snowden
Eamon Somers
Lynne Somerville
Emma Southon
Ingrid Spencer
James Spencer
Stephen Spencer
Ellen Spertus
Adamo Spilletti
Rachel Spink
Justin Stach
Laura Stafford
Anouska Stahlmann
Sara Stark
Jaime Starr
William Start
Henriette B. Stavis
Charlotte Steggall
Gaia Steinbuch
Katherine Stephen
Poppy Steward
Tabitha Stewart

Martyn Streeting
Alice Stringer
Deirdre Sullivan
Ryan Sullivan
Anne Summerfield
P Summers
Alice Sutherland-
    Hawes
Isla Swindells
Deborah Swinney
Harry Sword
Katie T
Phil & Sue Taphouse
Claire Taylor
Georgette Taylor
Rosamund Taylor
Sam Taylor
Charlotte Taylor-Page
Howard Teece
Sharlene Teo
Phillip Thelen
Jeffrey Thomas
Louie Thomas
Priscilla Thomas
David Thompson
Susan Thompson
Gillian Thorne
Rebecca Thorne
Timothy Thornton
Melodious Thunk
Georgie Thurlby
Jennifer Tighe
Janet Tindall
Rosa Tomalin

Roy Tovey
Emrys Travis
Nikki Traynor
Dave Treadwell
Josefina Troncoso
Else-Marie Trønnes
Adelaide Tsu
Rebecca Tucker
Jojo Tulip
Lee Turner
Lydia Turner
Matt Turner
Ian Tuton
Wendy Tuxworth
Rebecca Tye
Lewis Tyrrell
Mira Valk
Fiona Valpy
Anneke Van Belle
Amy van de Laar
Ariane van der Steldt
Esmée van der Weide
Laura van Dijk
Zach Van Stanley
Gemma Varnom
Janet Vaughan
Lauren Vevers
E. K. Victor
Sally Vince
Sanne Vliegenthart
Hannah "Eroo"
    Waddilove
Krysia Waldock
Imogen Walker

Steve Walker
Aoife Walsh
Conor Walsh
Eleanor Walsh
Lily Walwyn
Sami Wannell
Alex Ware
Caro Warner
Freya Watkins
Nicola Watkinson
Lizzie Ann Weathered
Ed Webb
Sue Weedon
Ange Weeks
Weird Beard
Becca Weiskirchen
Natalie Weizenbaum
Heather Wells
Westminster School
    Library
Gaby Weston
Jo Whaley
Tim Wharton

Charles Wheeler
Adam White
Gillian White
Harry Wilcox
Susan Wilde
Catherine Williams
Eley Williams
Klaussie Williams
Pip Williams
Tamsin Williams
Tim Williams
Tina Williams
Amy Williams (Tomes
    with Tea)
Emily Wilson
Penelope Wincer
Brooke Winters
Judith Wise
Nastassja Wiseman
Hugh Mee Wong
Edmund Wood
Peter Wood
Annabelle Woodger

Stacey Woods
Steve Woodward
Madge Woollard
Jo Worgan
Becca Wright
Bradley Wright
Hannah Wroblewski
Susan Young
Harry Yrrah
Noam Zackon